Henry Sturcke
Fooled into Thinking

Fooled into Thinking

Dylan, the Sixties, and the End of the World

Henry Sturcke

Photo on back cover by Edeltraut Sturcke
Photo on front cover by Henry Sturcke

ISBN 978-3-033-06138-5 (hardcover)
ISBN 978-3-033-06137-8 (paperback)

Prelude

Sunday, shortly after noon in the Catskills in August 1969. An irregular column of young people straggled along a road half-blocked by abandoned cars in the tired, haze-filtered sunlight.

I was one of them, a slender 21-year-old clad in a pale blue chambray shirt and jeans. My eyes, as pale as my shirt, took in the sight through plastic tortoise-shell glasses. My shaggy light brown hair was shorter than that of many ambling alongside. A canvas backpack from an Army-Navy surplus store held a new Nikon camera, which served as my ticket to the event, my reassurance that I was merely there to observe; I was in the midst of what was happening yet not a part of it. In addition to the camera, the pack held a second lens, a few rolls of film, and two steak sandwiches on rye bread.

My press pass for the festival was good for the entire three-day weekend. Why then was I among the last arrivals, shortly after noon on the last day? It was not for lack of interest.

The day before, I had been in my home state, New Jersey, attending Sabbath worship services of a strict, Bible-believing group living in expectation of the end of the world. A group into which I had been baptized less than four months earlier.

What was a member of a fundamentalist sect doing at Woodstock? Or, to turn the question on its head, what was a baby boomer rock fan doing in a conservative apocalyptic church?

To approach an answer to this two-sided question, let's go back six years, to another event that helped define the young lives of those born in the U. S. A. in the aftermath of World War II.

Chapter One

I sensed that the school intercom had been switched on, though we heard nothing at first save the hollow sound of dead air with a faint hint of white noise. Why the interruption? A Friday afternoon announcement from our rigidly-laced principal? No, the silence continued another second or two, then the sound of a radio feed, breaking into mid-sentence: "... we can confirm that the president has been shot." My first thought was of French President de Gaulle, who had been the target of assassination attempts over the Algerian War of Independence.

The illogic of an interruption of the school day for news from another country didn't strike me. We continued listening to the newsfeed, and I realized that this was not news from France, but from the heart of our nation, Dallas. We listened and grew numb: our president, John F. Kennedy, had not only been shot but was dead.

We stood, stunned, in the kitchen lab. Bob, Bernie and

3

I shared the first cubicle in from the doorway for our class, Boys' Cooking. We stared at each other in silence. Class dismissed, we spilled into the hall with all the other pupils to return to homeroom; the remaining minutes of school were canceled, as was sports practice.

My fifteen-year-old mind tried to make sense at the same time as two hundred million others throughout the country reeled in shock. I cycled in a daze to my dad's delicatessen in the center of town, where I stopped most days on my way home from school; I hoped routine would help at a time like this. The workers and customers there couldn't make any more sense of it than I. The repeated thought in my head: Lyndon Johnson president? The savage caricature on a then-popular comedy album, *The First Family*, had fixed his personality in my mind as that of a Texas yokel, scorned by the sophisticates of Camelot.

You might assume that, as a teenager, I was a Kennedy fan, but I wasn't. Nor were many in my suburban town across the Hudson River from Manhattan, beyond the chemical plants that lined the bay. When Vance Packard defined "bedroom community" in his study, *The Status Seekers*, our town, Westfield, was his example. An hour's commute took you to the city, either through the Lincoln Tunnel to midtown or the Holland to Wall Street, where the fathers of many of my classmates worked.

Westfield had polished its image in the previous decade.

A new municipal building went up, containing the town hall, police station, offices, and a public library, all modeled on the recent, Rockefeller-financed renovation of Williamsburg. Before that, the most distinctive architecture belonged to the many shambling wooden Victorian homes with gables and capacious porches, the ones that frightened Charles Addams decades before on his way home in fall and winter evening darkness as a boy, a trauma he spent a lifetime exorcizing in his cartoons of the lugubrious Addams family. But now, our town styled itself as "colonial." The next town to the north, Springfield, could even boast of being the site of a Revolutionary War battle.

Growing up in a "colonial" town helped spark my precocious interest in history. By the time I was in the third grade, I could recite the names of all the presidents in order, with their terms of office. This feat contributed to my playground nickname of "professor," a name I strove to disown.

During the campaign in the fall of 1960, I had been in the cheering crowd when Richard Nixon came to visit our town, speaking from the war memorial, a pillar in the center of a traffic circle. He had pledged to visit all fifty states during the campaign—Alaska and Hawaii newly admitted to the Union, and voting for the first time—rather than focus his efforts on swing states. There was no danger that Westfield would not deliver a safe majority to him, but there he was, the first presidential candidate since Theodore Roosevelt in 1912 to pass through. His campaign slogan "experience counts" resonated with me. Kennedy seemed callow, a millionaire's son who had rarely shown up for roll calls in his brief time in the Senate. His wife's breathy intonation led me to believe she was vapid. Though indifferent to the glamor of Camelot, I didn't hate him, yet I was aware that many in the country did. In the shock of that Friday afternoon in November, I remembered with revulsion the emphatic remark of an uncle during an otherwise friendly lunch at our table a few months earlier: "Someone ought to shoot that S. O. B." He was an investment banker, a national officer in a veterans' organization, and shared the sentiment of many of his Manhattan friends.

The sickening realization that this was not surprising added to my shock. Still numb from the news, I continued home, grabbed a Coke and descended to the basement. There, in a half-finished recreation room with thin plywood panels covering the cement walls I had established my lair, my realm. The alternative would have been the bedroom shared with my younger brother, Ken, with whom I got along as well as two boys, three-and-a-half years apart, with a disabled sister between, do. That twelve-by-twelve-foot room seemed as full as a warehouse, crammed with two matching sets of furniture: two beds that could be stacked bunk-style, but were not, plus wooden furniture from Sears Roebuck, bought unfinished, stained by our dad with our help: two dressers, two desks with chairs, and four small bookcases, two of them corner units. No matter how we arranged them, it was crowded.

Then there was the family room, paneled in tongue-and-groove knotty pine, added to the back of the house a couple of summers earlier. Bookcases lined one wall, but two other walls of shelving disappeared from the plan to make room for oversized ranch oak furniture, a piano, and a second television. My sister Edith might be practicing the piano. She and Ken might be watching two different TV programs, one in the family room, one in the living room. And our mom was prone to walk in and break my concentration with some question or thought.

So I spent my time in the basement, also filled with books—Dad never had enough room for his books. The glass-fronted wooden bookcases he had bought as a bachelor before going to war were down there. They had been in our bedroom before we got our matching sets of furniture. While dropping off to sleep, I gazed at the book spines—the pioneer and Indian on a survey of American history, the burning baggage train in the snow of the dust jacket of *War and Peace*—and wondered what mysteries they contained. There was a homemade bookcase in the living room, behind Dad's recliner, stepped-down to fit in front of the staircase. There were shelves and boxes in the attic, another refuge he had outfitted for himself when I invaded the basement.

Aside from the bookcases, the basement room had a large desk, salvaged when one of the tenants in the offices upstairs from the store had moved out, and an old sofa, relegated when my parents bought a new one for the living room. My two guitars were there. One was a cheap Sears model, with a plywood top and high action guaranteed to dampen the motivation of any aspiring musician. The other had been bought that spring at a pawn shop in Macon while on the family's biannual vacation to visit Mom's grandmother and other relatives. Though also made of cheap wood, this guitar was different, in ways that mattered to me. There was no manufacturer's name on the head; it had the anonymous aura of a drifter. It wasn't stained, but painted. The dark brown was chipped in places, revealing the raw wood underneath. It smelled of ten thousand cigarettes. The nut had been filed down, and two additional grooves incised; evidently a previous owner had experimented with doubling the top two strings. It was a guitar with tales it mutely refused to tell: they could only be teased out by playing it.

The cavernous metal desk under the one small high window had a door on the left that hid a spring-loaded stowaway shelf, meant to store a typewriter, but I had a better use: an old portable record player. It had three speeds, so that it could play 78s, as well as 45 rpm singles and 33 rpm records—long-players (LPs)—that contained fifteen minutes or more of music on each side. My collection began at garage

8

sales, where I bought stacks of scratchy old singles. Now my allowance went most weeks for a new LP. New or old, they all sounded roughly the same after a few plays on that machine with its primitive, worn needle.

I can't remember a time I didn't respond strongly to music. Margie, my mother, filled in the time before memory began. She only had to turn on the radio to keep me content while she did housework; she told me how I would circle with a limp-eared stuffed rabbit under one arm, thumb in my mouth, the other hand clutching a blue blanket and fingering the satin edge. "How Much Is That Doggie in the Window?", "If I Knew You Were Coming I'd Have Baked a Cake," and my favorite, "Irene Goodnight." Occasionally, she placed a shellac disc on the whirling platter of the console in the living room, where it spun at a dizzying 78 revolutions per minute. These records were mostly party music such as the "Liechtensteiner Polka," imported from Germany. But music came to me not only from recordings. The exaltation of processionals and recessionals from the church organ, the fluty calls of birds in the morning and their droning chatter as they settled for the night in the woods that edged our backyard, even the whine of the wind through the television antenna cable running down the side of the house next to our bedroom window and the polyrhythms of the heavy mixer in the bakery of Dad's store as it slapped twenty-five-pound batches of dough: all these and more called to me.

This basement room was my refuge that November weekend in 1963. For the next seventy-two hours, I shared in the shock of a nation, going up to the living room at times to watch the continual reportage, collective grief therapy. Live coverage—including the murder of the presumed assassin—interspersed with repeat views of earlier developments, especially Friday's motorcade in the late autumn midday sunshine. I spent hours transfixed, watched as Air Force One touched down and the coffin was carried out, speculated on whether the Russians had anything to do with it, but there was a limit to how much I could endure, so I distracted myself with two other preoccupations.

One was my record collection, but Buddy Holly, Del Shannon, and U. S. Bonds didn't sound the note of relief. Instead, there was another record that I repeatedly played over the next three days: Bob Dylan's *Freewheelin'*. My friend Marc had given it to me a couple of months earlier; I had played it, but it had made no impression. Peter, Paul and Mary's rendition of Dylan's "Blowin' in the Wind" had been a hit that summer and their blended, three-part harmony made it one of my favorites on the radio. Marc's uncle was their arranger. He had given Marc's parents the Dylan LP with the recommendation: this is the next Woody Guthrie. His mother gave the record one listen, said, "this is not Woody Guthrie," and told her son to get rid of it. It was natural that he gave it to me, since we, together with two girls from nearby Cranford,

Barb and Lynn, were working up a folk quartet.

I must have seen Dylan on television toward the end of the summer, when I watched the civil rights march on Washington. None of the three networks broadcast it, but a few independent stations around the country did, among them channel five in New York. The singers, actors, and actresses who performed quickly faded from memory, but Martin Luther King, Jr.'s "I Have a Dream" speech made a deep and lasting impression. Until then, I had shared in the bland assumption that it was a free country, but that everyone had his or her place, with "liberty and justice for all," in the words of the pledge I had repeated every morning in grade school. King's eloquence and the force of his argumentation probed the cracks in my complacency. If I had been in front of the television when Dylan sang, I didn't remember it.

But now, on that long November weekend, his were the words, his was the voice that spoke to me. I responded to all the songs in varying degrees, but especially to "A Hard Rain's A-Gonna Fall," Dylan's apocalyptic recasting of an old British ballad, "Lord Randall," in which an anxious mother questions her roving son. On the surface, the "rain" seemed to refer to nuclear missiles raining down from the sky, but I quickly realized it was not a simple equivalence. Like all well-crafted poetry, the symbol was potent, recalling Noah's flood and all the disasters ever since, as well as those I and others feared were about to come.

My other distraction, to supplement listening to Bob Dylan, was to pore over *The Plain Truth*, a primitive-looking magazine that cross-bred religion and news. It had started coming to the house every month about a year earlier. In fact, two copies had arrived of the first issue. A customer in Dad's store had told him of it, and my dad, Charlie, became curious. Charlie was an intellectually restless man, a farm boy with a vivid intelligence that had been thwarted by family and international events in the 1930s. Well- and widely-read, he was given to challenging the accepted wisdom on almost any topic. His customer told of a series, "The Plain Truth about the Protestant Reformation," that aroused his interest. Meanwhile, my maternal grandmother, a religious hobbyist in Florida, had been reading the magazine, sent some copies north, and urged her daughter to subscribe.

I had become aware of the magazine but hadn't given it much attention. In a house flooded with books and magazines, its dated look held no appeal, a black-and-white photo on the bottom two-thirds of the cover, a simple logo centered on the top third, with a pale salmon border, like a decades-old issue of *Time*. The text inside, set in three columns, made heavy use of capitals, italics, and exclamation points. Titles of the articles made frequent use of words such as "now," "crisis," and "revealed." It warranted more than a passing glance when in the summer an issue arrived with a cover photo of Charles de Gaulle and an article on the Common Market, an interest of mine. I noticed, yet in the summer there were too many other things to do, so I set it aside again.

Now it was different. Like Dylan, *The Plain Truth* offered a voice that seemed to make sense when nothing in the world did. I scoured the house, not only the dusty stacks on both sides of Charlie's recliner but also in piles that had migrated to the attic in one of Margie's desultory spurts of cleaning. I separated back issues from the other magazines, book club prospectuses, and unopened solicitations, and like a squirrel gathering nuts for winter, added the unearthed finds to my hoard in the basement.

Each issue began with an editorial by Herbert W. Armstrong, who seemed self-important, infected by Babbitry and boosterism, but with some life to his writing. In one issue, there was an article by Roderick C. Meredith, entitled "USA Riding to Total Collapse in 20 Years." There was no mention that it was a reprint from five years earlier; I would learn in time that "five to ten years" was a rolling concept in Meredith's worldview. In spite of the sensational style, though, the basic premise seemed plausible. I had been born into a world in turmoil, when the West lived in what was called a cold war, toe to toe with what seemed to be a monolithic communist bloc. In periodic drills in elementary school, we prepared for a nuclear attack by crouching under our desks with arms over our heads and practiced looking down, training ourselves to suppress the urge to look out a window to catch a flashing glimpse of a mushroom cloud.

Those years seemed idyllic in retrospect, though, after the Berlin Wall went up in the summer of 1961. A year later, in October 1962, the news that Soviet missiles armed with nuclear tips were on their way to Cuba brought a new height of tension. For a few days, it was as if the nation's entire population held its collective breath. At the peak of the uncertainty, I went for a walk after school in the woods behind our house. The beeches, birches, and oaks were normally my outdoor refuge, a counterpart to my indoor nest in the basement. There I came across one of my schoolmates, a neighborhood boy two classes ahead of me. We hadn't interacted much before, but now we had something in common: Bobby evidently had the same need I did for a peaceful clearing. We exchanged a few words, something in the vein of "so long, it's been good to know ya;" there was no need to express the possibility that we might not wake to see another day. One of the side effects of living in the suburbs of the greatest city in the world was knowing that we were doubtlessly among the targets of any first strike from submarines in the Atlantic, or long-range missiles soaring over the North Pole.

As if the news from the mainstream media were not dramatic enough, there were the interpretations from sources that claimed to be more patriotic: The Red Threat, these claimed, was internal, too. Schools were undermined, the

14

State Department riddled with traitors, the Federal Reserve Bank was a threat to the economy. So the scenario depicted by Meredith and other *Plain Truth* writers fit what I had heard before, except that a new source of information was added: They claimed to know this on the basis of biblical prophecy. Parts of the Bible with which I hadn't been familiar despite years of Sunday School and confirmation lessons, Daniel and Revelation, were heavily referenced, cross-checked with an apocalyptic speech ascribed to Jesus shortly before his crucifixion. And all of it tied into the present, according to the claims of the purveyors of *The Plain Truth*. I couldn't know it at the time, but this was all part of Herbert Armstrong's second try at predicting the end of the world. He had gotten his start in the 1930s, when depression and dust bowl convinced many Americans they were living in the last days. He added to this a fixation with European dictatorships. Hitler, he was confident, was a side distraction. The real threat was Mussolini. He knew this from his interpretation of prophecy.

At a time when there was a general feeling that old structures were breaking down and the future seemed uncertain, to come into contact as a fifteen-year-old with men (all the authors of *Plain Truth* articles were male) who claimed to have the answers was alluring. All the more so since they didn't claim this on their authority, but on something that seemed objective: ancient prophecy, recorded for two thousand years in the Bible, but now coming to life, in our day.

15

Another article carried the categorical title "Russia Will Not Attack America!" (whew). Nevertheless, America would be attacked, but by the same powers it had fought in the first two World Wars. And it would lose World War III (oh no!).

Most of all, I was drawn to articles by another frequent contributor, Herman L. Hoeh, who specialized in historical topics with an esoteric slant. He wrote on arcane questions: Where did the twelve apostles go? Where were the lost ten tribes of Israel? Hoeh also wrote about Germany, the country of my ancestry on my father's side, the land my dad had left in 1935 and to which he never returned.

I read these words less than twenty years after the end of World War II. Doyle Dane Bernbach had recently revolutionized Madison Avenue with an advertising campaign designed to make a German product loveable, the Volkswagen. Their success didn't reach everyone: the parents of many of my schoolmates categorically refused to buy one. There was a general feeling that the heralded denazification after the war had been carried out half-heartedly in a rush to make the western half of Germany a bulwark against Soviet advance. Rumors of Nazi leaders who escaped to friendly South American countries abounded. So when I read in *The Plain Truth* that Hitler was hiding there, too, planning his comeback, it didn't strike me as inherently implausible.

My feelings toward Germany were ambivalent. My dad was born there, in the middle of a triangle of flat land between the Elbe and Weser Rivers, between the cities of Hamburg and Bremen, one of six surviving children of a man who had emigrated to the U. S. in the nineteenth century as a teenager and taken out citizenship on the first day he was eligible. But then he returned to Germany to marry and take over the family farm, one that had been the family home as far back as written records go—five centuries—and who knows how long before that. He was proud of both citizenships and passed his love of both Germany and America to his children. I try to imagine his feelings when the U. S. entered World War I in 1917 and draw a blank; I never asked my father, but then again, he was an infant at the time. In politics conservative, my grandfather shared the feeling of many of his compatriots that Germany would not have lost the war had it not been betrayed, in the common phrase of the time, knifed in the back. Conspiracy theories abounded, but he drew the line at Hitler. While some of his children found Hitler a charismatic figure, he made no secret of his dislike. He died in 1931 and was spared having to witness Hitler's accession to power.

Charlie was fifteen when his father died. He and his younger sister were the only children left with their mother in Germany, the older siblings having already emigrated to the U. S. The farm had been sold to settle debts his brother John incurred when his grain mill failed. Charlie was a loner. Precociously gifted, both in all things mechanical as well as

17

in his classes, he was allowed to skip the last two years of primary school to enter a boarding school in the next town, but was required to learn on his own the material he had thereby missed out of books the family had to purchase. He was one of the few who did not board at the school. There was one other from his village, a distant cousin who was the village teacher's son, but Charlie was a farm boy. So in addition to not fitting in very well with the other children in his village, he was also an outsider at his new school.

He spent his meager pocket money on books, leaving just a little over for pastry. Natural science, exploration, history, even literature interested him. When his older brother Harry took Hesse's *Steppenwolf* out of his hand and read the dedication, "nur für Verrückte" (only for the crazy), he passed it back with the sardonic remark that it was the right book for Charlie. His intellectual curiosity, which made him a stranger to his contemporaries, caused his parents to have hopes for him. His father wanted him to become a doctor, his mother, a pastor, a wish shared by the local pastor, who gave him a copy of Schleiermacher's *Über die Religion*, which I still have on my shelf, when he was confirmed.

One interest dwarfed the others: astronomy. To the end of his long life, Charlie never lost a sense of wonder that the universe exists. But as the orphan of a bankrupt farmer, his only hope of studying was if he could win a scholarship, such as the one open to all pupils in Prussia offered by the chemistry giant, I.G. Farben. Charlie placed second, good enough for a stipend to the Hannenhausen Institute of Technology (now integrated into the University of Hannover). It was a work-study grant; he would have to be a lab assistant to one of the professors, who was doing some of the early work on plastics.

His plans changed however just before graduation. His oldest brother Herman, on a visit from America, wanted to reunite the family by bringing him over, as well as his sister and his mother. Herman informed the director of Charlie's school, and countered the latter's protests with the question, "how much do you earn?" His scoffing reply to the director's disclosure: "I make more than that in one week slicing bologna."

And so it came to be that I was born in the U.S. My dad's departure, though bitter for the loss of his chance to study, was made lighter by his distaste for the National Socialist government. In the two years since taking power, the party had embarked on a program of subverting all the institutions of society (the paradox of a party that comes to power by democratic means but is not democratic). The man who was director when Charlie entered prep school was out. In his place, his sadistic deputy, who wore the correct button in the lapel of his jacket. The new *Gauleiter* for the area had called a mandatory assembly on a Sunday morning as soon as he took office; one man, a wounded WWI veteran, decided to go to church instead. He disappeared for a few weeks, and after his return told of where he had been. Charlie scorned anyone who later claimed ignorance of the existence of concentration camps.

Within days of graduation, Charlie boarded a ship for the U.S., his mother and sister had left previously, leaving him behind to finish. On the other shore of the Atlantic, he was met at the pier by his brother Harry, driven to the delicatessen (the same one he later bought and in which I grew up working), and handed an apron. When Charlie spoke, in Low German (*Plattdeutsch*), his brother cut him off curtly: "You're in America now; we speak English here."

Yet the German heritage within the family remained; Charlie's siblings all married other North Germans, he was the only one who didn't. My memories of family parties when I was a child are of a cloud of *Plattdeutsch* floating overhead as I played with my cousins. It was the sound of a family of strong personalities, fiercely loyal, warm and loving. At the same time, there was no mistaking their pride in living in America, suffusing the old-country virtues of hard work and thrift within the American dream. Something the Third Reich *redux* Meredith warned of was going to destroy.

With time I noticed in *The Plain Truth* a stress on obedience to the Ten Commandments as the solution to the ills of individuals and society. As with the Nazi threat, this was inherently plausible. I had been brought up Lutheran, and memorizing the Decalogue, together with Luther's brief explanations of each commandment, was part of preparation for confirmation. By the time I began reading these magazines, however, two years after confirmation, I had thrown away my childlike beliefs and was radically questioning everything, including the existence of God.

To say I was brought up Lutheran oversimplifies. The family faith for the previous four centuries had been Reformed, the church of Zwingli and Calvin, which had small pockets in northern Germany. Charlie's mother, though, was the granddaughter of a newcomer to the village, from closer to Hamburg; that family was Lutheran. So now, in the U. S., the entire clan, an umbra around my Oma, supported a Lutheran congregation. The fact that Reformed congregations in the U. S. tended to be Dutch, rather than German, was an additional factor. Before the mobility brought on by World War II and its aftermath, many denominations in the U.S. ran along ethnic lines, aiding in the assimilation of immigrant families. Even the Lutherans in the U. S. grouped themselves along ethnic lines. Many German-Americans were, like my family, part of the Missouri Synod, the most conservative of the Lutheran groups. They were the first mainstream denomination, for example, to popularize young-earth creationism, the view that the earth and life on it were only a few thousand years old, previously widespread only in fringe groups such as the Adventists.

Until adolescence, I had enjoyed church, dressed up in the latest of a series of three-piece charcoal suits handed down from my cousin Carl, Herman's son. A highlight of the day was the joy of seeing my "twin" cousin, Louise, sitting with her and her family in one of the polished oaken pews, often the one with a brass plate with my grandfather's name (my name as well). Louise was born six months after I was, the daughter of Charlie's younger sister, Alice, known to the family as Tante Mudel. At that time, her parents and mine had apartments in houses facing each other on 6th Street in Plainfield, the town in which we were born, so for the first two years, we were inseparable. After that, each family bought a house, but in different, neighboring towns, hers in Scotch Plains, mine in Westfield. From then on we saw less of each other, making Sunday, when we met at church in Plainfield, a highlight of the week. Beyond that, I enjoyed Sunday school, especially the lessons with an elderly widow who also babysat me, my sister, and my brother on the rare occasions our parents went out. Our congregation was raising funds for its own building; until then, it met in the church of the Seventh-Day Baptists. It never occurred to me at the time to wonder why that congregation didn't use it on Sunday morning. That's something I found out later, when I also found out this was the national headquarters of that small denomination, and that the bearded worthies who looked down on our Sunday school lessons from their portraits on the wall—they reminded us children of the faces on the package of Smith Brothers cough drops—were earlier denominational leaders.

I enjoyed worship services and singing the hymns. There was a children's choir, and until my voice broke, I sang a solo, the second verse of "Silent Night," each year in the Christmas service. The Lutheran hymnal was filled with strange melodies from the sixteenth and seventeenth centuries; only later did I realize their unique sound came from modalities that were neither the major nor minor that most Western music used, modalities soon to turn up on the radio, when the Beatles incorporated them into their blend of many musical influences.

While my formal religious training was Lutheran, Charlie took it upon himself to make me aware of the Reformed tradition as well, talking at the dinner table of Zurich reformer Ulrich Zwingli. The tale of the failure of Luther and Zwingli to understand each other the one time they met was in line with Charlie's general insistence that there was another side to any story; at the same time, it created in me a feeling that there was a hidden substratum to who I was. In fact, I was heir to another religious tradition as well. My mother, Margie, came from Georgia and had been brought up Southern Baptist. The biannual family trips to her grandmother, whom we called Granny, and to the house in which Margie was born, were always at Easter time, and exposed me to a worship style that contrasted with the formal Lutheranism in which I was brought up. Egg hunts at dawn in the early morning dewy chill, followed by Easter services in a clapboard country church, with a rollicking piano thundering accompaniment to a packed congregation lustily intoning "He Arose" and other hymns, capped off by a potluck lunch at which Granny's chicken pie was extravagantly praised: all this went into the mix of the religion that I was rejecting at age fifteen. One more strand: the Methodism of Granny's widowed sister, who lived with her. She told of another of their sisters, who had died when I was five. She had married one of the Candler brothers. Another was a Methodist bishop; the third bought the Coca-Cola recipe from the Atlanta druggist who concocted it; a generous portion of the resulting fortune went to Emory University and its Candler School of Theology.

Lutheran, Reformed, Baptist, Methodist: when a *Plain Truth* article decried the many denominations, saying they all couldn't be right, and asked, "Where is the church Jesus founded?", the question made sense.

The existence of God, anxiety about the future, the true church: These were issues that would play themselves out in the coming months and years, but the groundwork was being laid during that long November weekend in those hours of immersion in the world as seen by this obscure magazine.

Chapter Two

The ordeal ended with the televised funeral on Monday, and we returned to school on Tuesday for two days of classes before the long Thanksgiving weekend. The routines of dressing, gathering up textbooks, walking from class to class offered a glimmer of hope that life would continue as before.

But the world had changed, and so had I. Over the next few months, I set out to convert my schoolmates to the cult of Dylan. Like most missionaries, my lot was ridicule and rejection; some conceded they liked one or two of his songs, but only when others sang them. When our English class took up modern poetry, each pupil had to present a poem of his or her choice; I took *Freewheelin'* to school and played "Hard Rain." The strongest reaction was from the teacher, who stood in front of the class as if transfixed and murmured, "the imagery . . ." I was perplexed: a teacher more hip than the pupils?

I guardedly kept my other new interest, the doomsday scenarios from *The Plain Truth*, to myself, except for some needling criticism of the unexamined premises of those around me. Outwardly I conformed, continuing to go to services with my mother, whose own interest in church had been rekindled by my childhood love of it. After my voice broke and I was too old for the children's choir, I became an acolyte, lighting the candles before services. Pastor Van Steen, who confirmed me, retired a year later, after serving the congregation since ordination in the early 1920s. His successor came to this, his first pastorate after teaching Greek at a seminary, and provoked controversy for what seemed to be innovations. Only later did I learn that much of what he instituted was standard Lutheran liturgy; Pastor Van Steen had been more influenced by Reformed ways than I knew, perhaps one reason why the family felt comfortable with him. One innovation of the new pastor was the use of crucifer to lead the procession at the beginning of services. As a long-serving acolyte, I was one of those chosen for the new role. This brought informal contact with Pastor Dodge before and after services, as his office, to the side of the sanctuary, also served as the vestiary.

One day after services, as we divested, I asked him a question. I had been surprised to read in *The Plain Truth* that the word "hell" in the New Testament had been used to translate three discrete terms in Greek, each with a different reference, yet the pictures associated with these words had merged into one concept of hell in the popular imagination. To test the reliability of what I read in this magazine, I asked if it were true. Happy to see my interest, Pastor Dodge took a Greek New Testament off his shelf and showed me passages with each of the words, *Hades*, *Gehenna*, and *Tartarus*, explaining what they meant—the grave, a fiery pit, and a subterranean place of restraint, respectively—in terms that corresponded with what I had read. Why didn't he preach this, I asked; he replied, "Oh, that wouldn't interest anybody." Well, it interested me. I didn't know at the time that Pastor Dodge was from Eugene, Oregon, where Herbert Armstrong had begun his ministry, and had been a classmate of Garner Ted, Herbert's son. He shared his recollections of the under-sized boy from the wrong side of town with patched jeans and a chip on his shoulder with my aunt when she consulted him about my new enthusiasm, but I only learned this years later. Would it have made a difference to me then?

In addition to my part in worship services, I continued attending Sunday school. The class for teenagers met before services in the organ loft. The teacher became increasingly irritated with my pointed questions, questions that none of the others posed. Finally, he burst out in exasperation: "Well, if you don't believe that, you're not a

Lutheran." So that was that; from then on I felt free from the need to consider myself Lutheran.

Meanwhile, our folk quartet continued to practice sporadically, but toward winter's end other sounds distracted me. One day in early February I walked through town after school with some soccer teammates. We stopped on the slush-rimmed sidewalk in front of The Music Staff, the town's record store, to scoff at the photo sleeve of a new 45 featured in the window, each of us topping the other in macho remarks about the mushroom haircuts. Nevertheless, I tuned in to see the Beatles on *The Ed Sullivan Show* that Sunday night. I wasn't an instant convert, but there was something infectious not only about their music, but also the personalities they projected.

Still, when I neglected my homework it was to practice songs from *Sing Out!* song collections and Oak instruction manuals: two volumes of folk guitar by Jerry Silverman, and two books by Pete Seeger, *How to Play the Twelve-String Guitar Like Leadbelly* and his banjo book (by now, a used five-string stood next to my guitars). I bought a collection of Woody Guthrie songs and a couple of his LPs. The songs were easy to pick up, often two chords, almost never a fourth chord, and I sang them for hours. I borrowed Carl Sandburg's *American Songbag* from the town library, as well as a Lomax collection of cowboy songs, and a well-worn copy of Harry Smith's *Anthology*, six LPs of music collected

28

from old 78s that were transmissions from a strange, distant land, the past.

At school, I joined the folk music club, and older boys were generous with tips and encouragement. I also sang in the glee club and took voice lessons from the music teacher who was the choir director. That was my introduction to the *Lieder* of Schubert, which I came to love as much as Dylan's songs, sometimes even more. I was reluctant to practice for these lessons at home, though. Ever since the combination of my voice breaking and my discovery of music on the radio, I had been imitating the singing I heard there. Now I added the intonations of Dylan and the other folkies. Charlie asked in irritation: "You used to have such a good voice, why do you have to sing like that?" My defense was, that's just how my voice sounded now. To practice "Who is Sylvia" at home would blow my cover. Then I discovered that I could study the sheet music in silence at home, and when I sang in my lesson, it was as if I had practiced. This trick of mental imaging worked in other ways as well, as I learned over time.

I also spent the winter on the track team. I had joined the first soccer team our school fielded that fall, as second-string goalie for the junior varsity, and a teammate encouraged me to come out for track. In other schools, the sport was called indoor track; not at ours, since the team trained outdoors in every weather on a circular residential street near the school; there was no through traffic, so we were undisturbed. I enjoyed the discipline and the camaraderie. The retching and the stomach cramps the runners called stitches seemed like a rite of passage. The pranks in the locker room afterward and the loudly-sung "Arrivederci Roma" in the scalding showers were a comic counterpoint. Not enough speed for sprints, not enough endurance for distance runs, I trained as a quarter-miler, a compromise decision.

Our first meet was at the Armory in Jersey City. For most of the way I was in the middle of the pack, but when I saw the finish line, I succumbed to the thought, "It's nearly over." Coach Clarkson, on the sideline, saw what was happening and repeatedly shouted, "Don't let up!" to no avail as several runners passed. I learned that day to mentally trick yourself, to focus on a point beyond the finish line, so that you run through it. It was not enough to make me a track star, but it has helped in many other situations, and was another insight into the mind's mystery.

School dictated much of my time, but little of my interest. This despite placement in advanced classes from the time I started junior high. In the seventh grade, there was an accelerated science program, part of the American response to the Russian launch of *Sputnik*, the first human-made satellite. The school also started extracurricular Russian language classes after school; I still remember some.

Lectures and demonstrations from working scientists from chemical companies along Newark Bay enriched science class, and we took a field trip to the Brookhaven National Laboratory on Long Island, at the time a center of research in nuclear physics. The charts we brought home— one of the table of elements, the other depicting the spectrum of radio and light wave frequencies—fascinated me, and I hung them on the wall in the basement. Still, I was not a gifted scientist, to the disappointment of Charlie, who like many fathers hoped his son would live the life he had failed to achieve. My approach to science was more that of a poet; I shared the sense of wonder that animated my dad. I was intrigued, as I gazed at the chart on the wall, that light and sound are different sections of a continuous spectrum and wondered what it would be like to hear color or see sound. Unfortunately, this didn't translate into the grades Charlie expected. Taking part in the accelerated program did have a long-term advantage, though. We took biology a year earlier than most, putting me on track to finish my science requirements sooner, thus leaving room in my schedule to add a second language, French, along with the German I had started in the ninth grade.

Vague career goals flitted through my imagination. In elementary school, I couldn't decide between President of the U. S. and a baseball player. In junior high, I thought of becoming a history teacher. A student teacher noticed

31

my interest and sat with me in the school lunchroom to encourage me. Later a new possibility took shape, journalism. In my childhood, the waning of the golden age of daily newspapers, New York still had three serious papers that appeared each morning, although the *Herald-Tribune* was losing ground to the *Times* and the *World-Telegram & Sun* was on its last legs. The Hearst-owned *Journal-American* came out in the afternoon, just in time for the commute home from the city, and there were three tabloids, the *Daily News*, the *Daily Mirror*, and, in the afternoon, the *Post*. Radio journalism was also at its zenith, upholding the standards set by Edward R. Murrow. In the summer just before starting high school, I read a memoir by one of "Ed's boys," William Shirer's *Berlin Diary*, his eyewitness account of Hitler's rise. I thought it would be romantic to become a foreign correspondent, and reasoned that a second foreign language wouldn't hurt my chances.

Along with German and French, I took Plane Geometry, English and American History. My practical elective was Boys' Cooking. I had never been good in "shop," and since Charlie was the better cook in the family and made his living in the food business, I wanted to learn about it. In English and History, I was still with the advanced placement group and enjoyed the class discussions in both, which made up for the fact that my avid reading seldom corresponded to the assignments.

I had begun to read before entering kindergarten, as Charlie coaxed me to decipher the words in the balloons over the heads of comic figures in the three Sunday newspapers he brought home every Saturday night. I soon progressed to Golden Books, slim volumes with board-bindings, watercolors on every page, and simple words. The same publisher issued stamp books on various topics with sheets of perforated stamps to lick and paste on the appropriate page, where I found relevant text and a line drawing; my cardboard box with a jumble of broken crayons was never out of reach.

At the newsstand, rifling through boxes of comic books on the floor below the magazine racks, I discovered, behind Superman and the Green Hornet, a selection of Classics Illustrated, my introduction to *Ivanhoe*, *The Three Musketeers*, *Uncle Tom's Cabin*, and other stories. I was getting used to finding what interested me hidden in the back, stuffed behind what interested others. I made weekly trips to the library, first to a Carnegie-funded building close to the center of town, then to the new library, closer to home, when the faux-Williamsburg municipal building opened. I carried as many as I was allowed to check out, taking care not to trip where the sidewalk—concrete paving slabs laid end-to-end—buckled and cracked where tree roots underneath pushed the surface up. I concentrated on volumes of such series as Childhood of Famous Americans and Landmark Books to supplement those I received as Christmas or birthday presents. I even read the occasional adult book, if the topic interested me enough. One was Jim Bishop's *The Day Lincoln Was Shot*, which I turned into a play for our fourth-grade class, casting my crush, Deborah, as Mary Todd Lincoln, to sit beside me (her family moved that summer, the first of many heartbreaks).

When allergies led to weekly visits to Dr. Schillinger for my four injections, I discovered copies of *American Heritage* in the waiting room, to which my dad soon subscribed. That led to direct-mail offers from their book division—richly-illustrated volumes on the Revolution, the Civil War, and other topics—as well as the chance to become charter subscribers to a companion magazine, *Horizon*, which covered art history. When the newest issue of each arrived, I was the first to rip open the mailing box and pore over each page. Sometimes my curiosity led me to look up the related article in the many volumes of the World Book that Charlie had bought for us. When an Encyclopedia Britannica salesman came to call, I stretched out on the living room carpet, and leafed through the sample volume he produced from his bulky valise. Charlie bought not only it, but the new Great Books of the Western World set as well, each with a bookcase.

Given my voracious reading, I'm mystified that the appearance of a title on an assignment list was enough to sour me on the thought of reading it. A few years later, I came across Paul's agonized musing on human nature in his epistle to the Romans ("that which I ought to do, I do not"), surely part of the answer. Perhaps another is the quality of some of the highly-esteemed works ("Breathes there a man with soul so dead, who never to himself hath said . . ."). But it seems as if there was another factor, my suspicion that "the truth" was extracurricular.

The days passed with classes, sports practice, our folk quartet rehearsals, guitar and banjo practice in the basement, and a monthly dose of *The Plain Truth*. I added Dylan's first and third LPs to my collection. They were recognizably by the same performer who had recorded *Freewheelin'*, but each was distinct. The first, simply entitled *Bob Dylan*, with a close-up photo of the baby-faced singer, featured only one of his compositions to supplement the exuberant folk, country, and blues songs he played. The third was called *The Times They Are A-Changin'*, not only the title of the opening track but a summary of the overall theme. The songs were for the most part explicit protest songs, some tied to topical incidents, such as the violent deaths of Medgar Evers and Hattie Carroll, others more general. The face on the cover photo was no longer chubby. Instead, dressed in a chambray work shirt, he looked more like Woody Guthrie than he would in any other photo. The guitar parts on both were simpler than those on *Freewhee-*

lin', and I worked them out by ear and added the songs to my growing repertoire.

The days lengthened, and I began looking forward to summer. The previous summer, when I was fifteen, I had worked in Charlie's delicatessen, putting in a 48-hour week (six eight-hour days) for $50. I quickly learned the prices of all the baked goods, including the discounts when bought by the dozen, and only rarely had to check the big list of sandwiches and their prices hanging high on the wall behind the front counter. On Sunday, the store closed in the middle of the afternoon, earlier than the other six days of the week, but there were housekeeping chores before going home. The worst involved taking all the baked goods out of the glass-fronted cases and carefully sweeping out the crumbs. As the newest employee, the task was mine, and being the boss's son didn't get me out of it.

Another task, though, gave me exquisite pleasure: the ritual of making coffee. Charlie took pride in serving the best coffee in town and approached the job like a chemist, a method he passed on to me, one that took care with ingredients and process. A double-vaulted urn stood behind the sandwich counter, each vault holding two-and-a-half gallons. The key, Charlie stressed, was to start by cleaning the urn before brewing each fresh batch, then scrubbing it thoroughly once a day. Otherwise, he explained, oil from the beans stays behind and turns rancid—a taste

I learned to recognize in the many coffee shops, restaurants, and church social halls that don't take the same care my dad did. Next, Charlie stressed the quality of the beans. The small difference in price between good and indifferent coffee beans is minimal compared to the difference in taste when a pound of them is brewed into two-and-a-half gallons of coffee. The quality of the water was important, too—the store had its own well—as well as the temperature; the water should nearly boil, but not quite.

Throughout the summer, I put $45 each week in a college savings account (Charlie matched each dollar saved, an incentive), and kept $5 for pocket money. Most of my free time had been spent with two friends, John and Jeff, as we trained in hopes of joining the football team when we started high school in the fall. During the first week of practice, I heard about the new soccer program and raised my sweaty face from the dust to switch to a sport with the prospect of staying on my feet.

But the summer of 1964 would be different. I had always been curious about life in Germany, my father's homeland. Charlie had never been back after leaving in 1935, but his siblings often spent summers there. Tante Mudel was planning a trip that summer with her husband George and their two children, including my twin cousin, Louise. I was welcome to join them. My brother Ken had spent the previous summer at a camp in New Hampshire with Louise's brother Ed, but summer camp held no interest for me. A trip to Germany was another matter. Yes, I wanted to go.

But the plan was tentative. Oma lived with Louise's family, and her health declined through the winter. If she lingered, the trip was off. I had mixed feelings when she developed bronchitis and had difficulty breathing. In early April, she died, and the family finalized plans for the trip.

Oma was 82 and had been a widow for more than thirty years. She was fifteen years younger than her husband, and not yet fifty when he died. From that time her fiery energies were devoted to her children and grandchildren. It was largely her indomitable will that kept the family together in central New Jersey. Family holidays were big occasions. Easter—ham with green beans and mashed potatoes—in the home of Tante Mudel and her family. Thanksgiving—turkey with all trimmings followed by pumpkin and apple pies—alternated between our home and the lakeside home of Charlie's older sister, Tante Tiene, and her family. For Christmas with its roast beef, we gathered at the home of his oldest brother, Herman. There was often a summer party as well, either at our home, or Tante Mudel's, or Tante Tiene's at Lake Mohawk. After steak from the grill with corn on the cob and *Schmorkartoffel*—sliced potatoes that were first fried with bacon and onions, then covered and softened by condensed steam—, followed by blueberry cobbler and ice cream, the adults sat in the gathering dusk and talked in a satisfied mix of *Plattdeutsch* and English while we children chased fireflies.

My memories of Oma are different from those of the older cousins. They still experienced her as the dynamo she had been. I'd been told by the old-timers that she didn't walk between chores on the farm, but trotted. I recognized this because of the way Charlie hustled in his store, undoubtedly in emulation. Apparently, she could deliver good tongue-lashings as well, something that Tante Mudel learned from her. But in my memory, she was mild like a dormant volcano. When she came to visit, Margie had to bring out all the socks that needed darning; Oma was content to sit and chat, but only if her hands could stay busy. She seemed a benevolent eminence, whether seated at the head of the table at family parties or sitting in the pew with us at Sunday services. She spoke no English, or even many words at all, except for *god* (*Plattdeutsch* for "good," pronounced like the English word "goad") as a word of approval, or *och ne* ("oh no!") as dismay.

This mild quietude contrasted with my other grandmother, Margie's mother, who was twenty years younger than Oma and still a bundle of temperamental energy. Grandma came of age after World War 1, in many ways an example of Fitzgerald's "new generation." From a small town in central Georgia, she had gone taken the unusual step of going to college, took a degree in music, and worked at times as a musician, at other times, music teacher. Along with a college poetry anthology, I still have her crumbling sheet music. An early marriage ended in divorce when Margie was two; my mom carried only one memory of her father through life: he had come to pick up his two daughters for a visit shortly after the divorce; her older sister got in the car, Margie—out of fear, perhaps a confused sense of loyalty to her mother—refused. She never saw him again, nor did I ever meet him, so that I grew up with strong memories of two grandmothers, and even one great-grandmother, Granny, but no grandfathers. I seemed to look for substitutes for that role. The first was the Jewish doctor I often saw for my nearsightedness and my allergy shots. Perhaps part of the attraction of Herbert Armstrong, editor of *The Plain Truth*, was his ability to project himself into this role as well.

Grandma was headstrong, opinionated, with a voracious appetite for life. She was in her third marriage, to a Jewish accountant. His work for an oil company took them for long postings to South America, where she learned Spanish. Her frequent, newsy letters, typed in a white heat, mistakes impatiently struck over or left uncorrected, in a voice by turns chatty and querulous, kept the family informed of her travels, her quarrels, and her ailments. I thought no one in the world wrote like she until I read the letters of Flannery O'Connor. It must have come with their Georgia upbringing.

She was also enthusiastic in her religious interests. In addition to being the first in the family to subscribe to *The Plain Truth*, she was a fan of Assyrian Christian George Lamsa and his claims that the Syriac translation of the Gospels shed light into the Aramaic language and culture in the time of Jesus. As with Charlie, the unorthodox held more appeal for her than the orthodox. And while most of what I heard her play on the piano were old southern hymns, from time to time she broke into the ragtime and stride she played in her youth. I sensed the dismay of her mother, Granny; although I revered her, this silent censure made the unprogrammed interludes more delectable.

Another passion of hers was family history, which coincided with my general love of history. This was another interest that came from both sides of the family. Charlie had documented his family and Grandma, Margie's side. In neither case was the interest dispassionate. Charlie had to compile his family tree for a school project back in Germany, one aim of which was to discover which children didn't have proven Aryan descent. Grandma, on the other hand, had felt looked down upon by the family of her first husband, Margie's father, with their descent from the F. F. V.'s, the so-called first families of Virginia. These self-designated first families did not claim chronological primacy, but social, from the time Governor Berkeley sought to recreate the aristocracy of England on the shores of the New World in the time of their eclipse in England during Cromwell's protectorate. In reaction to what she felt were slights, she was eager to show that her family had equally valid claims, something she went to her grave maintaining, with only dubious evidence.

As a child, I listened eagerly to her tales of ties to the Clark who explored the Louisiana Purchase, of the Armisteads, who were on the scene at many crucial events in history, even to a supposed descent from Pocahontas. For a history-obsessed child, to grow up believing that he was descended from such, as well as "probably" distantly related to General Lee and "certainly" to Mary, Queen of Scots, helped make history for me, in contrast to most of my schoolmates, a living memory, rather than a dusty recital of dates and names in the pages of dryly-written books.

Charlie's dinner-table tales of his family matched those of Grandma's for romantic flair. The family had always been prominent farmers in the area, so-called Vollhöfner, which meant they had a full-sized farm, both an economic and a social distinction. Marriages were with the other families of that class. Behind that was an even more stirring tale. The family name was not German, but Viking. These raiders, traders, and explorers had ranged far—from Odessa and Constantinople to the east, and to Iceland, Greenland, and likely North America to the west, arriving long before Columbus. This, too, contributed to my sense of a secret identity, hidden under the unassuming Dobie-Gillis-like life of a storekeeper's son.

These family tales were enriched as I continued to read *The Plain Truth*, whose articles about the lost ten tribes and the legendary destinations of the twelve apostles were based on the adherence of its writers to the theory of British-Israelism.

This ancient myth was a form of the general feeling of Anglo-Saxon superiority rampant on both sides of the Atlantic in the twentieth-century. The conviction of being a special people—whether in the sense of John Winthrop's "City on a Hill" or as an empire upon which the sun never set—rested not only on economic and naval power but even more on a presumption of moral excellence.

British-Israelism added to this general view the tenet that the ten northern tribes of Israel had migrated to the northwest from their Assyrian captivity, indeed that the Assyrians themselves had wandered away from their homeland. I had heard about the migration period when the western half of the Roman Empire decayed and collapsed. In the reconstruction conveyed in *The Plain Truth*, the tribes that collected in central Europe, loosely referred to as German, had begun their migration as Assyrians.

43

Those that moved further north and west, to Scandinavia and the British Isles, were the good guys, the Israelites. To support this, Hoeh and fellow authors offered homespun etymology, such as the deciphering of the term Saxon as "sons of Isaac." So it was this, rather than raw materials, fertile land, technological innovation, or political and economic ideals, that accounted for the rise of the Anglo-Saxons. It was all a result of divine providence—acknowledged in a general way by many non-adherents of this teaching.

It turned out that this was the particular ingredient that set aside the people behind *The Plain Truth* from the many other purveyors of prophetic interpretation. They shared, I was to discover in time, an application of these old texts to current events in the Middle East such as the Balfour Declaration of 1917, the establishment of a Jewish state in 1948, and—in a few years time, in 1967—its takeover of the old city of Jerusalem. But they went further. If one accepted the premise that Bible prophecy was a roadmap to the present day, then their argument that God surely could not have failed to mention major nations such as the U. S., the Soviet Union, and Germany while lavishing meticulous attention on less significant nations such as Jordan and Ethiopia was plausible. Unique to *The Plain Truth*, then, was the extension of prophetic significance to the United States and other lands far from the eastern Mediterranean. This notion was the basis of their confident prediction that a resurgent Germany, at the head of a United States of Europe, would be the power that would invade the U. S. Who else could do it but the latter-day Assyrians? Germany had indeed remarkably recovered far more quickly and vigorously than anyone expected less than twenty years earlier, in 1945. More reason for my ambivalent feelings about the German half of my heritage.

Perhaps I came to this fascination honestly, almost genetically. Margie's clearest childhood memory of her maternal great-grandfather, a Civil War veteran with twinkling blue eyes and a snowy white beard, was of him seated in a rocking chair with three items in his reach: a radio, a globe, and a Bible. Whatever was reported in the news he sought to locate both on the globe and in Bible prophecy.

My interest in history spilled over into politics and current events. This, too, may have made me ripe for the approach of *The Plain Truth*, like my great-great-grandfather, a newspaper in one hand and a Bible in the other.

In Westfield, being politically interested usually meant being Republican, despite the fact that one of the state's two senators, a Democrat, lived there, in the exclusive circular residential island that served for winter track practice. Margie's family, though, had been Democrats, like most of the unreconstructed South. After she married, she dutifully cast her ballot for the same candidates Charlie did, so as not to cancel his vote, she reasoned. My political views at first were inherited, then veered from far left to far right in my adolescence. In that winter of 1963–1964 I was active in the local youth chapter of the Republican party, the TARs (Teen-Age Republicans), even holding an office, constitutional secretary. With the others, I attended a state convention that would cast a straw vote for the upcoming nominating convention. A tense day; many delegates from other towns were for Nelson Rockefeller, then governor of next-door New York, but he was too liberal for our chapter. Our hero was Barry Goldwater, a conservative, but not your grandmother's conservative. Instead of a stuffy, Wall Street-connected isolationist, Goldwater was modern, a jet pilot, hi-fi enthusiast, from the West. His libertarian streak contrasted with the rigid moralism of other conservatives we had known. His shoot-from-the-hip rhetorical style appealed to us as well. Despite our vocal and energetic efforts, though, we failed to carry the day. The majority of the delegates, as expected, went for Rockefeller, but the defeat was temporary.

That day held not only disappointment but disillusion as well. Some real-life elected state officials were there, whom we were eager to meet. But by the time we did, it was evident the Solons had been more interested in partaking of the well-stocked bar than in meeting us. My political education was beginning.

Meanwhile, my enthusiasm for Bob Dylan continued

unabated. But just who was he? Robert Shelton's notes on the back cover of the first LP told a romantic tale of hardship and extensive travels, yet seemed somehow to strain credulity. Who was this guy? Was he just putting everyone on? Some whispered that his name wasn't really Dylan. In those pre-internet days, gathering information wasn't easy. Research skills the school librarian sought to instill didn't yield much beyond Shelton's rave review in *The New York Times* from 1962 for a then-second-billed act, opening for the Greenbriar Boys, as well as a short notice in *Time*, with their characteristically overblown yet snarky tone.

The growing interest in the folk boom led to specialty products in the media. One was a magazine tied into the *Hootenanny* television program. Dylan had refused to appear on the show, along with many others, in protest over the continued blacklisting of Pete Seeger, who ironically had first made the term "hootenanny" popular. Still, the magazine ran a cover photo of Dylan at Newport in the summer of '63, blue chambray shirt with rolled-up sleeves, seated next to Joan Baez. This confused me; what happened to the chubby, sweet-faced girl hanging on his arm on the cover of *Freewheelin'*? But the profile inside didn't add much to still my curiosity.

More help was the sound of the three LPs themselves, but here, too, the indications were contradictory. The unadorned sound of a single folk guitar, strummed or finger-picked, supplemented by a wild, careless, but somehow effective harmonica told an honest tale, as did the laconic tone of his delivery. But then there was the inconsistent, fake-sounding "folkie" enunciation. Even the sound of his voice varied from LP to LP, sometimes even from song to song, yet always striving to seem older than his years. Was this the real deal, or a put-on? Or was that the message: that the real deal is a put-on? This intersected with my education through the pages of *The Plain Truth* that there was a hidden, ignored meaning behind the surface appearance of our day-to-day world. I became a callow, fifteen-year-old cynic.

Dylan's message fed into this as well. Beyond the vague tales that passed for biography and the contradiction in the sound, what drew me back repeatedly were the words. Sly, all-knowing, sententious and humorous by turns; in later years it would be forgotten how funny Dylan was. Living under the threat of nuclear war, his response was by turns caustically judgmental ("Masters of War"), apocalyptically poetic ("A Hard Rain's A-Gonna Fall") and funny, as in the mangling of a Lincoln quotation segueing into "I'll let you be in my dream if I can be in yours" ("Talkin' World War III Blues"). There were other protest singers making their mark, but he transcended by approaching his subjects indirectly, not topically. Yet even when he did take an incident from the daily newspaper, his lyric moved behind the surface, as in two songs from his third LP, *The Times They Are A-Changin'*, "Only a Pawn in Their Game" and "The Lonesome Death of Hattie Carroll," in which he not only decries senseless killings but examines the psychology of the killers. Even a title such as this last one seemed of another time, like something from a broadside sheet. *Broadside* was the name of a magazine that published many of his first songs, as well as those of Phil Ochs, Tom Paxton, Len Chandler, Buffy Sainte-Marie, and others. I bought a collection containing many of these, among them songs Dylan had written, but not recorded. Although only a few months older than those on his records, their finger-pointing simplicity showed how quickly he assimilated the stance of the Greenwich Village scene he had joined, then rapidly left behind.

By then I was trying my hand at creating songs and poems. I can no longer say when I started, but can remember struggling over staved-paper in grade school, trying to notate music I heard in my mind. A little later, listening to the radio, I made up "answer songs" in my head. Answer songs were a sub-genre, especially popular in country music, such as when Skeeter Davis answered Jim Reeves's hit "He'll Have to Go" with "He'll Have to Stay," or when Jo-Ann Campbell answered Claude King's hit with "I'm the Girl from Wolverton Mountain." These were mostly formulaic, sometimes even using the same instrumental track, but they were exercises in learning to look at almost any situation from the opposite point of view. I never set any of mine down on paper. One of my first written poems was about the Kennedy assassination, contrasting the shot from behind to the old days out west, or at least the movie version, of a sheriff and his challenger facing each other at high noon on the street. It was sophomoric, but after all, it was my sophomore year in high school. More texts followed, mostly dealing with one of two topics: the mournful laments of a love-sick teenager and soapbox proclamations from one who had the answer to everything.

None of these went into the repertoire of the quartet. I didn't show any to them or anyone else at this point. Our sporadic rehearsals hadn't led to any performances, other than at a community center on the poor side of town. Ours was a rec-room combo.

After Oma's funeral, plans for the summer trip finalized. I went to a photographer's studio for a passport photo, sent off my application, then went to the family doctor to begin the series of typhoid and yellow fever shots required for a trip to Europe. On the way home, I stopped at the Music Staff and bought a two-LP album, part of *Lead Belly's Last Sessions*, a set I'd been eyeing for a while. Part of the pleasure of those pre-CD, pre-Amazon days was the time spent in record stores, flipping through the bins, looking at the jacket photos, reading the liner notes, taking first one out to purchase, then putting it back and deciding on another instead.

I took my new purchase home, and since I had the house to myself on that Friday afternoon, opened the console stereo in the living room, placed the first side on the turntable and lay down on the sofa to begin to listen. In the course of the four sides of the set, the reaction to the shots set in. No one told me I could have taken an aspirin to minimize the effect. Instead, I lay there, Lead Belly's heartfelt moans echoing my mental and physical state. It passed in a few hours, but the effect of the music lasted. I felt I was getting closer to the mother lode, the source of all that music expressed about life.

The spring days lengthened, and summer approached. At the end of the school year, our folk quartet went to a party. It had a farewell feel. One of the two girls in the group, Lynn, was moving to Ohio with her family once school was out. Marc and Barb were off in a dimly-lit corner of the basement recreation room, as they often were. Lynn and I ended up on a couch, where I had my first kiss. She may have been working up to it for a while; if you're in a quartet, your best friend is the girl of one of the two guys in the quartet, and the other guy has no girl, it seems like the logical outcome. But that she waited until the end of the school year, just before moving away, speaks of ambivalent feelings. She had her family drive by my house a

51

couple of days later to say goodbye; we never heard from each other after that. My mind was already on board ship and heading for Europe.

Chapter Three

When I take that first passport, issued in anticipation of the trip, out of my memory drawer, I already know what I will find when I leaf through it. There is the large blue blotch from a pen that leaked during a flight. There are the visa stamps, some faded, some smudged, some so crisp you can almost feel the impact of the stamper. And then there is the photo. It shows a teen who had successfully shed his baby fat but had not succeeded in taming his hair. My pale eyes look warily at the camera through the half-wire frames popular in the early sixties; my striped tie is fashionably narrow.

Early on Saturday evening, June 20, my dad made room among the tools in the trunk of his white Buick Elektra for my bulky suitcase. Then the family got in for the drive to the pier on the Hudson River on the west side of midtown Manhattan, where the TS *Bremen*, the pride of the Norddeutscher Lloyd shipping line, was moored. There we joined the rest of the clan gathered around a large table in the first class dining room, organized by Charlie's oldest brother, Herman, who was also making the crossing with his son Carl. When the call came for all non-passengers to disembark, I felt a twinge giving goodbye hugs to Margie and Charlie, my sister Edith and my brother Ken, and staying on board with Tante Mudel, Uncle George, their children Louise and Ed, as well as Uncle Herman and Carl. Soon the pilot tugs started, and the boat glided from the pier just after midnight. We remained on deck as the liner slipped under the lights of the newly-opened Verrazano-Narrows Bridge connecting Staten Island and Brooklyn, then only a few lights glimmered starboard from Long Island, otherwise nothing but ocean and dark sky, so we settled into our cabins. Ed and I shared one; Louise was next door with an au-pair girl returning home.

In the coming days, Uncle Herman occasionally snuck us up to first class, other times we just went and used his name when challenged. I was free of envy, though, for even tourist class offered endless delights in those sunset years of the fabled Atlantic crossing, when a European vacation began and ended with a week's stay in a floating five-star hotel. In those days, few flew across the ocean, a situation that would soon reverse. Norddeutscher Lloyd gave up this route just seven years later, and the *Bremen* was resold and renamed many times until it was finally towed for scrap. In a final act of dignity, it escaped that fate by breaking free of its tow line to sink in the Gulf of Aden.

That was an unimagined future as the *Bremen*'s bow sliced the waves. Heading east in a stately progression of twenty-three hour days, we settled into a dreamy routine regulated by four trips a day to the dining room. Breakfast was not very different from what I expected, though I doubt I ever had a grilled tomato with my eggs and sausage before, but lunch that Sunday showed me what awaited us each day: a choice of nine appetizers, then soup, an entrée of either fried mackerel or smoked ribs, with four vegetables to choose from on the side, as well as potatoes, followed by apple cake with whipped cream and fresh fruit. For a sixteen-year-old boy with a healthy appetite, it was pure delight. The obligation of first returning to our cabin to don a jacket and tie was a small inconvenience.

We sampled the activities, shuffleboard and ping-pong on deck, an indoor pool and gym; even the lifeboat drill interested me, although I wondered if there were enough boats for all of us. A movie theater featured three showings a day, on alternate days English- and German-language. But watching the passengers, such as the old men playing chess in the library, mustache and fingers stained yellow from years of cigarettes and cigars, afforded a better show. It even took days to tire of the endless variation of waves and feeling the wind graze my skin and lift my hair.

As darkness settled each day, we descended to the ballroom. Carl was gracious about having his younger cousins tag along to join the college-age crowd around him. His dark eyes and slim grace on the dance floor meant he could choose from many partners; I danced with them as well.

Louise and I often took the guitars we brought on deck in the afternoon or to a bar in the evening. I was awkward with girls, too self-conscious to dance gracefully, despite Carl's best efforts to teach me, but was learning that a boy with a guitar often has listeners.

After nearly a week at sea, we sighted land. First stop, Saturday morning at first light, was Cherbourg, then across the Channel to Southampton, followed by a stately cruise past the white cliffs of Dover. The next afternoon the ship berthed at its final port, Bremerhaven, Germany. I gazed at the glistening terminal and wondered who had lost the war. The docks we had left in New York had seemed decrepit, adding the odor of decaying wood to the other smells from the slow river; the facilities on this side of the Atlantic gleamed with self-confidence. Despite the efficiency the terminal exuded, it took a little longer than normal to leave. Uncle George had stocked up on coffee and cigarettes in anticipation of the many visits to an assortment of relatives. He saw no need to declare that he was well over the duty-free limit, which led to a very careful inspection of all our suitcases and an expensive fine.

Finally, we passed through the frosted doors to the reception hall where Fritz, youngest son of Uncle George's sister, waited. He drove us to the family farm, a few miles down the road from Charlie's home village. The excited chatter in Plattdeutsch on the way freed me to take in the sights of village and field through the half-hour drive. After settling in and sitting down to supper, Louise, Eddy and I tagged along with Hinni, Fritz's oldest brother, who had recently taken over the farm from his father, as he went to a field to check on their cattle. Here, too, just as when we first arrived at the farm, it felt strange that the earth wasn't swaying when I got out of the car. My legs missed the roll of the sea.

We soon fell into the rhythm of helping with the chores, whether on our knees, digging potatoes bare-handed out of the earth, or gathering dried peat from bogs and tossing it onto a tractor-towed wagon, then into the loft, where it dried further. These dried bricks of peat were still the primary source of heat for the house, and the earthy smell of peat smoke combined with the flavor of everything we ate. Once I even plucked a freshly-slaughtered chicken after it had been dunked in a pan of scalding hot water, though more experienced hands than mine removed the innards. The quills that I saved as a trophy were forgotten within days, and didn't make it back to America.

I enjoyed all of it, except for the first chore after rising. The aroma of the soiled straw from under pigs to place on the compost stayed with me for years. I imagine it was done first to get it out of the way, making the rest of the day more enjoyable, though arduous. Still, I wondered more than once if it were worth getting up to face this.

We had arrived just after the solstice, and at a latitude further north than my hometown. It seemed never to grow dark. The weather was also a change from the hot, humid summers I endured but didn't enjoy in New Jersey. A typical day offered fifteen minutes of sunshine, followed by fifteen minutes of rain, succeeded by fifteen minutes of clouds, repeated in an endless cycle. I shielded myself from temperatures in the mid-forties when we left for the fields in the morning by dressing in two undershirts, a flannel shirt, and a sweater, topped with a jacket. By mid-afternoon, the temperature could go to the upper fifties, and I worked shirtless under the vast sky that stretched in every direction over the flat land, unencumbered by the many buildings that commonly surrounded me.

It was the height of strawberry season, and we ate them in various ways four times a day, the last serving with vanilla pudding in the soft light of the long summer evening. Just when I dreaded sitting in front of another dish, the strawberries were finished, and the cherries had ripened, so the routine started anew. In all we sat at the large oil-cloth covered table near the peat-burning stove six times a day: first for bread and butter with coffee after cleaning the pigsty, then a full breakfast of eggs and fried potatoes after the rest of the morning chores, then out to the fields, followed by a return for a midday dinner. More work or errands, such as delivering potatoes to the naval academy in Bremerhaven, until coffee and cake in the afternoon—one of the simplest cakes, called *Botterkoken* in *Platt*, was one of my favorites—then a supper of cold cuts and cheese, and before bed, fruit and pudding. At supper I suppressed the urge to make a covered sandwich, learning to eat open-faced style, with a knife and fork. I tried to follow the talk at the table as well as I could, but *Plattdeutsch* was not like the German I had taken in school for two years by that time, and I often had only a vague notion of what the others were saying. Eddy, Louise and I were our own best company.

The summer was not all work; we made the rounds of family throughout the area. Especially memorable was a family party in Charlie's hometown. The long central hall, the *Diele*, had been set with trestle tables, offering fifty places. Uncle Herman took over cocktail-duty, as he did wherever he was, whether the host or a guest. This evening, his Old-Fashioneds had packed their usual wallop, so when it was time to make a second bowl of strawberry punch, and he retired to the kitchen to mix it, in his lubricated state he reached for the salt instead of the sugar.

Fooled into Thinking

The bowl went to its place of honor; we eagerly dipped our punch glasses in, drank, and immediately headed for windows and doors to spit it out. That punch was legendary, so that decades later, becoming reacquainted with people who were there that evening, there was an immediate kinship. We were members of the Fellowship of the Salted *Erdbeerbowle*. There was something nearly sacramental in having shared it.

I created another legend when we visited a farm across the road from the old family homestead, that of Uncle Johnny and Tante Leni. Their older boy had a motor scooter, and we all took turns riding it; mine ended unceremoniously with a crash into a bush of stinging nettles. Tante Leni immediately brewed a pan full of chamomile tea and washed the scratches as well as she could, but the itch remained for a couple of days. In nearby Bederkesa, we visited Tante Henni's bakery. She was one of Charlie's favorite cousins, now a widow. She had four children, two boys, Egon and Heino, older than I, and two girls, Marion and Elke, who were closer to my age. They took their American cousins swimming in an outdoor pool in their town, a welcome afternoon.

Louise and Eddy had taken riding lessons at Watchung Stables, near home, and they didn't want the entire summer to go by without riding, so Uncle Lüer, Uncle George's brother-in-law, arranged to borrow a horse, said to be a riding horse, from another farmer. The horse had a stubborn temperament. On the day it arrived, Eddy was kicked but not badly hurt. I took a turn holding the reins while Louise got the saddle ready, and decided that horses are smarter than they let on, though in a crotchety way. It planted its front hoof directly on my right foot. Although my heavy work boots shielded my toes to a degree, it was distinctly uncomfortable. Having seen what the horse did to Eddy, though, I let the horse keep its foot wherever it wanted. Louise, undeterred, mounted and rode away. Some time later, she returned on foot, scratched and bruised. She had been thrown, the horse had run off, but was found and taken back to its farm. My boots went home with another memento of the summer, a long deep scratch along the ankle from a barbed wire fence I didn't quite clear when I jumped it. My foot caught on the top strand, and the fence flipped me like an expert wrestler, leaving my foot up in the air, wound between two strands, while my head and shoulders were on the ground. If the others hadn't freed me, I felt, I might still be hanging there.

Despite the need to pack for an entire summer of varied activities, I had made room in my suitcase for a stack of *Plain Truth* magazines, along with three books. Two were paperback novels, my summer reading for school, the third was the Bible Grandma had given me for my confirmation. I began reading as-yet-unfamiliar parts, such as Leviticus, where I found prohibitions of certain animals. One was only to eat what chewed the cud and had a split hoof—which, I learned, was what the King James "cloven" meant. I had spent enough time among the livestock that summer to know that cattle were permissible, but what about pigs? I had seen their hooves; they were unmistakably cloven. They seemed to be chewing all the time as well, but what did it mean to chew the cud? I was not good at biology, so I asked Ed, who was. Sure enough, no pigs. I had stumbled across this bit of information at the most awkward time imaginable, partway through a summer with relatives of relatives, whose primary source of protein was supplied by pigs. Pork was served in every way imaginable, at every meal. Even the potatoes at breakfast and supper were fried in bacon and lard. I picked my way among the food as best I could for the remainder of our stay.

While I accepted the authority of the Bible, even the parts most Christians didn't practice, I was still unsure about the twist on current events in the pages of *The Plain Truth*. I observed, questioned, discussed, and concluded that Germany had indeed made a remarkable recovery in the nineteen years since war's end, and was the motor driving prosperity throughout Western Europe.

The family we stayed with had three sons. The oldest, Hinni, who now ran the farm, was already married and had a child. The youngest, Fritz, was a couple of years older than I, and doing his compulsory military service after an apprenticeship as an electrician. But I was especially drawn to the middle son, Hans-Peter. He had gone to the same nearby school that Charlie had attended, spoke English well, and was politically active in the Jusos, the youth wing of the Socialist party. On one of his visits home, the two of us talked long into the night, fortified by the half-liter bottles of beer Hans-Peter had taken from a cool corner of the barn on our way out into the garden. One of the allegations in *The Plain Truth* was that the vaunted denazification program after the war had been half-heartedly carried out and that there were many former party members throughout the schools, judiciary, industry and politics, a charge that Hans-Peter readily confirmed as fact. It didn't strike me at the time as odd that the politics reflected in the pages of the magazine aligned with the right wing of American foreign policies and domestic issues, but with the left of other countries such as West Germany. At any rate, we felt a kinship. When it was time to leave at the end of the summer, I gave him the paperbacks I had brought with me, *All the King's Men*, by Robert Penn Warren, *The Rise of Silas Lapham*, by William Dean Howells. I never saw him again; he died in a traffic accident years later.

Life on the farm was broken up by two ten-day trips. We took them in the new Volkswagen bus Uncle George had bought and would bring back to the U.S. to use as a delivery wagon for his store; even with the cost of shipping it across the Atlantic, this brought significant savings. For the import duties, it was considered used.

The first trip took us through other countries of Western Europe. First stop Amsterdam, with a ride through the canals, a tour of the Anne Frank house and visits to museums. At the Rijksmuseum, I purchased three prints mounted on beaverboard: a Vermeer interior, a cloudy landscape by van Ruisdael, a painter unknown to me before this trip, and a Rembrandt. I bought this despite my newly-sensitized disapproval of depictions of Christ, which to me were a violation of the second commandment. But this Jesus was in the background, dimly-lit, half-turned to look at Peter, vigorous in his denial of knowing him. In the half-century since, this picture has always been in my workroom in the many places I've lived. My talisman, an exhortation.

Another artifact of the summer is an album I assembled after returning home. A series of photos shows four of us with noticeably diminishing enthusiasm, finally sullen and glum, as we lined up in front of the landmarks we visited. At the Hague, for instance, posing in the drizzle for Uncle George's 35mm camera in front of the queen's palace, parliament, the royal gallery, and Madurodam, a miniature village with scale models of many of the public buildings of Holland.

Photos fix a moment, an expression. But memory

saves its own images, more truthful than a snapshot, for they record what stirred the imagination. From our stop in Brussels, I remember the contrast of the splendor of the Grand Place and the narrow streets we navigated on our way there with the unusual odor of chicory-flavored coffee and a haunting Near Eastern melody sung by an unseen woman in a rundown tenement. We drove to Waterloo, the site of the "close-run thing" that finally put an end to Napoleon's career, and climbed the 226 steps to the lion atop an artificial mound. In the peaceful summer afternoon, I tried to imagine the thousands of soldiers from seven nations. Napoleon had been a hero to many, an incarnation of the Beast of Revelation to others, and here, 149 years earlier, his fate had been narrowly decided. I thought of the coming danger from Europe foretold in the pages of *The Plain Truth*, in their telling, it would be the last revival of the Roman Empire.

We drove to Calais and boarded a ferry for Dover, enduring one of the worst passages the more experienced fellow-travelers could remember. It's still hard for me to enjoy the watery French vegetable soup we had for lunch. With my deep aversion to vomiting, I managed to keep it in, but Louise went to the rail six times. I clung to the rail next to her as the boat rolled from side to side. At the height of its arc, we looked behind us, and it seemed from our perspective the rail was lower than the sea beyond.

The crossing made the drive through the cultivated landscape of Kent seem all the more peaceful. The place names were familiar; they had been used as street names in the neighborhood between my house and the elementary school I had attended. Tante Mudel had planned the trip using *Europe on $5 a Day*, but put the book away when we got to London, knowing it was useless; even then, with the favorable postwar dollar rate, London was an expensive city.

No sooner checked in, we cousins went into the TV room, where we unexpectedly caught the Beatles performing both sides of their new single, "A Hard Day's Night" and "Things We Said Today." No lip-synching, this was live. Their film had just opened that week in a vast cinema, the London Pavilion, at Piccadilly Circus, and the three of us went. Not knowing any better, we were thrilled that there were still seats available in the front row. Despite the resulting stiff necks, the larger-than-life depiction enthralled us.

Alongside the new, we saw much of the old—Westminster Abbey, the Tower, Buckingham Palace, Madame Tussaud's, and on a day-trip, Windsor Castle—but none of this had the lasting impact of that movie. I could no longer divide music between folk (good) and pop (bad). Back on the farm, in the twilit evenings, we cousins sat close to the wooden-encased radio in the sitting room and carefully tuned until we found Radio Luxembourg. I liked almost everything I heard and began to slip out of my folk purism. The optimistic pop of the Beatles was irresistible, while the folk-blues roots of another group, the Rolling Stones, were unmistakable in their hit, "It's All Over Now." And number one for some weeks that summer was the Animals' recording of "House of the Rising Sun," scarcely rearranged from Dylan's recording of Dave Van Ronk's setting, just electrified, as well as drained of any subtlety. Admittedly, there was a lot of fluff as well: who else remembers the Honeycombs? Many of the groups proudly wore their indebtedness to Buddy Holly, whether in their name, such as The Hollies or the Searchers (the name of the movie in which John Wayne memorably uttered, "That'll be the day"), or the thick black horn-rimmed glasses on the singer in Freddy and the Dreamers. When I returned home and bought the first LP by the Rolling Stones, I found they had recorded one of Holly's songs, "Not Fade Away." A more subtle reference to Buddy Holly, which made it all the more satisfying when you got it, was the variant of the name of Holly's band, the Crickets: the Beatles.

So it was no shame that Buddy Holly was my first music hero. I had spent most of the spring of 1959 listening to the radio, shortly after "the day the music died." I had come down with measles, German measles and chicken pox in rapid succession. Usually, I would have read while confined to my bed, but was under doctor's orders not to, for fear of damaging my already myopic eyes. So Margie brought a radio from the kitchen to my room, and I tuned it to WABC from New York. My interest in history meant that one of my first favorites was Johnny Horton's cover of Jimmy Driftwood's "Battle of New Orleans," but I soaked in all I heard: Frankie Avalon, Bobby Darin, Fats Domino, Ricky Nelson, the Platters, Dion and the Belmonts, Connie Francis. To catch up on the back-story, I listened avidly to the Saturday evening "golden oldies" programs, featuring Chuck Berry and generous portions of Doo Wop. I soon felt an affinity to "the late, great" Buddy Holly, two of whose tracks, "That'll Be the Day" and "Peggy Sue" were often played. My favorite present Christmas 1960 was *The Buddy Holly Story*, an LP that collected some, but not all of his most successful tracks.

I went on to buy other LPs as they came out: the second volume of *Story*, then *Holly in the Hills*, a collection of early, country-inflected music he had done with a high school friend, Bob Montgomery, and finally a collection called *Reminiscin'*. The photo on the jacket, showing only a dark shadow in profile with his trademark glasses, was mesmerizing. The music inside raised more questions than it answered. In addition to his controversial, slowed-down take on Little Richard's "Slippin' and Slidin'" and a torrid version of Chuck Berry's "Brown-Eyed Handsome Man," nearly as good as the original, the set offered tracks he had cut at home on a tape recorder, shortly after his move to New York. Why did he write his saddest, most disillusioned songs just after his impulsive courtship and marriage to a secretary he met at a music publisher's office? He was dead; his widow wasn't speaking. Life was clearly more complicated than my young mind could fathom.

We left London, spent a night in Dover, and boarded the first ferry back to Calais, a crossing as remarkably calm as the trip over had been turbulent. Our drive to Paris was slow-going; in planning the trip we had failed to realize that progress through every village (no highways in those days, or perhaps they existed, but we wanted to save the tolls) would be impeded by the fact that we had chosen Bastille Day, July 14, to land. We could have gotten into the spirit of it and enjoyed the parades we were stuck behind, but we were on vacation, so we didn't have time to waste.

We finally reached Paris and did the things tourists do: we cousins climbed the 600 steps of the Eiffel Tower while the adults took the lift, oohed at the panorama at Sacre Coeur on Montmartre, were overwhelmed by the Louvre, and hushed at Notre Dame. On the banks of the Seine, I discovered the stalls of the *buchinistes* and filled my arms with purchases, both in French and English; among them a two-volume *Lincoln Day by Day*. The family went for a walk that evening; I stayed in and pored over my treasures.

We drove the next day through the countryside on a straight, poplar-lined two-lane road to Éparnay, home of Moët & Chandon. Uncle George, whose liquor store stood next to Charlie's delicatessen, had obtained letters of introduction from importers, so we had a private tour culminating in champagne and open-faced sandwiches under an ancient elm; our host assured us that Napoleon had been a guest under the same tree. After a stop in Reims and a visit to the cathedral in which the kings of France were crowned, with an equestrian statue of Joan of Arc in front, we spent the night in Sedan. I was expecting a metropolis since it had given its name to a luxurious form of transportation and was the site of the crucial battle in the Franco-Prussian War. Instead, it was a small town, easily traversed in a night stroll we cousins made with two English teenagers we met at our hotel. We exchanged addresses but still were surprised when the older of the two, a girl, sent Louise a copy of the newest single by the Beatles at Christmas.

I was beginning to get a feel for the fact that any spot of earth I might stand on, whether clothed in splendor or rags, is layered with the memories of the lives of those who lived before. Sometimes these memories are labeled "history," in the sense of entering books and school curricula. At other times, they are the memories of people we know. More often both individuals and events are forgotten, but their lives were just as real to them as ours are to us.

The second trip took us south through Germany, as far as Wiesbaden. The presence of a large American military base there meant the chance to indulge in things we missed. Although West Germany was closely aligned politically with the U.S., culturally there was a distance, wider than one can imagine now, fifty years later. So an evening of American-style hamburgers and ten-pin bowling, with American rock 'n' roll on the jukebox, was a little taste of a faraway home. Although I was hungry to soak up as much of the other, the European culture that was half my heritage, I reveled in it.

Our first stop had been Bremen, with its vast open market square lined by medieval and renaissance buildings, chiefly the cathedral and the town hall, with its statue of Roland, a legendary paladin of Charlemagne; the statue symbolized that a city had special rights within the Holy Roman Empire. In Cologne we felt dwarfed in the towering cathedral, in Bonn, we visited the Beethoven-Haus, where I bought a 45 rpm record of the *Moonlight* Sonata played on a restored piano used by Beethoven. My first sight of the Lorelei while driving along the Rhine, my first taste of ox-tail soup in Heidelberg, and stopping in the Teutoburg Forest on our way back north where, as I had read in German class, Hermann the Cherusker won a decisive victory over the Roman legions added to the store of memories that swelled in that summer.

In addition to the attractions that most tourists enjoyed, our itinerary was dictated by Uncle George's letters. As at Moët et Chandon, we had V. I. P. tours with liberal refreshments of Henkell Trocken in Wiesbaden, Asbach Uralt in Rüdesheim on the Rhine and the D. A. B.brewery in Dortmund.

The summer wound down with a visit to *Planten un Blomen*, the small, intricate park in the middle of Hamburg, and a round of *Schützenfeste*, the traditional marksman's fairs, at various villages. Uncle Herman entered in a nearby town and won, becoming that year's *Schützenkönig*. The honor of winning included buying a round for all the other participants, which may have discouraged some from taking their best aim. After the marksmanship, there was eating, drinking and dancing in a large tent. The band wasn't bad; perhaps they worked on their chops in some of the same clubs the Beatles played in during their Hamburg apprenticeship. In fact, one of their numbers was "My Bonnie," in the version Tony Sheridan had made popular—in Germany as least—with the Beatles as his backing band. The band also played a rousing German-language version of "Clementine," the name changed to Caroline.

As our return trip neared, we shopped for last purchases. Louise and I each bought a Beatles' LP; she the soundtrack from the film, and I *With the Beatles*, with its iconic photo of the four, their black turtlenecks blending with the background, so that their side-lit faces stood out. I also purchased a Beatle-like collarless sports jacket with leather trim at least two sizes too big, knobby wool in autumn colors.

On Sunday, August 16, we returned to Bremerhaven and embarked the *Bremen*. Once again, there was a farewell family party on board, but this time with the German relatives. A week of 25-hour days, as the boat sailed west more than 500 nautical miles a day, seemed to correspond to the languid, late-summer feel of a vacation reluctantly drawing to a close.We docked in New York on Saturday, August 22, and my first trip to Europe was over.

On the calendar, only nine weeks had passed, but our internal time-keeping works differently. I had matured much more than in any average two-month period. Not only had I been places that before had been but names to me, or unheard of, and met many people, it was the first time I had been away from my parents for more than an overnight. While I was not totally on my own, Uncle George and Tante Mudel gave me more leeway than they gave their children. Uncle George was good-natured, not as challenging and critical as Charlie, even toward his children, and Tante Mudel, though strict, seemed to have none of the fears and insecurities that hobbled Margie.

I was back home, still recognizable as the boy who left, and yet different in ways that couldn't be undone. Wher-

73

ever I had gone, whoever I had met, I asked questions, looking to confirm or contradict the articles I had read in *The Plain Truth*. Fascinated by assertions in the magazine that much of what passed as Christianity were ancient "pagan" elements, I had asked tour guides at every cathedral what had stood on the site before the present structure. After a short disquisition on the modifications of the current Gothic structure, and the Romanesque basilica that had stood there before, I finally got the answer I was expecting: long before Christians arrived north of the Alps, this had always been a sacred spot. I returned to the U.S. convinced that what I read in this obscure magazine was trustworthy.

Chapter Four

If the summer of 1964 had brought a growth spurt for me, it seemed as if the country I returned to had packed much in that short space of time as well, events of which I had only been dimly aware while away in those pre-internet days. There had been riots in Harlem, Rochester, Philadelphia, and while we were on the boat heading back, Elizabeth, just a few miles from home. President Johnson had used an incident involving a U. S. destroyer and North Vietnamese torpedo boats in the Tonkin Gulf to have Congress give him a free hand to use conventional military forces, even though he had not asked for a declaration of war; this opened the way for a massive increase in this "non-war." The Republican Party had nominated Barry Goldwater for president, and the campaign was gearing up.

Soon after returning home, I reported to the town's Republican headquarters as a volunteer, handing out leaflets and making phone calls. Here I saw another side of political life. I learned that political activists are often more radical in their views than most other folks; this is perhaps what motivates them to sacrifice countless hours in volunteer work. Although the party leadership forbade it, there were copies of a scurrilous LBJ biography under the counter, as well as *None Dare Call It Treason*, an early classic of conspiracy theory literature. They weren't on display, but if people asked for them, they could buy them.

Meanwhile, I was catching up on the issues of *The Plain Truth* that had arrived while I was gone. When the October issue came, its cover story asked: "How Would Jesus Christ Vote for President?" I was surprised with the answer: Jesus preached a government that was not of this world. He did not take a side in the politics of his day, so his followers should not in our day.

While a young person can hold mutually contradictory opinions, each of them extreme in its way, here I was confronted with a clear choice: continue my volunteer work or act in the way a follower of Jesus allegedly would. I was shaken but convinced. Perhaps the extremism of the backroom discussions at the storefront campaign headquarters helped. At any rate, I never went back. The payoff came in the mystified reaction of the other volunteers: I was a misunderstood non-conformist, proof to me that I was right.

I integrated this into the persona that developed that fall, the beginning of my junior year in high school. I hung a calendar print, a watercolor of the banks of the Seine in an autumnal drizzle, on the wall in the basement. I wore a black turtleneck for important occasions, such as my first date with the girl next door. She was two years younger, still in junior high school, so her parents had some misgiving about letting her go out on a date; *A Hard Day's Night* was opening in my town, and I wanted to see it again but didn't want to go alone.

Another element in this new persona was the new, non-political face of Bob Dylan, whose fourth LP, *Another Side of Bob Dylan*, had come out just before I returned to the States. The album was well-named. On one level, it seemed off-handed, as if to say: "Well, here's another Dylan record," which fit the sly delivery of the lyrics. But there was more. While the previous disc had been overtly political, featuring some of his most enduring protest songs, this one seemed its opposite. To call it non-political is not entirely accurate, but its focus was on the politics of sexual relationships, beginning with his insinuating desire to only be "friends with you" on the opening track, "All I Really Want to Do." The intended friendship was meant to be carnal but denied any attempt to remold the other or to possess in any other way than sexually. This song was book-ended with the closing track, "It Ain't Me Babe," in which the singer rejects any attempt of the other to remold him. Whereas the civil rights movement had been present throughout the previous LP, it seemed absent here, but only on the surface; civil rights and sexual politics merged in "Spanish Harlem Incident" and, possibly, "The Chimes of Freedom." Why did the lovers have to hide? From whom? It seemed as if the key to the whole collection was "My Back Pages," which sounded like his apologia for going missing from the civil rights marches, echoing my disappearance from the election campaign. The central trope, "I was so much older then, I'm younger than that now"—was it profound, or a poet's cheap trick of reversing a common expression to make it sound fresh? To me, it seemed more like the former. It suggested a letting go of a superficial maturity and embracing youth. Looking back to *The Times They Are A-Changin'*, its final track, "Restless Farewell," took on a deeper meaning, already signaled in its title, as if the singer, having demonstrated his mastery of the so-called protest song, was restless to move on. Not for the last time, it seemed as if Dylan the poet and performer were a chess-player, knowing the next move as he executed this one. The restlessness carried over to this LP, indicating that he would not be content to stay in this new place either. The torrent of words seemed at times sloppy, but more often surrealistically profound. The guitar accompaniment was often perfunctorily strummed, with pseudo-Spanish riffs on a couple of the songs. The uncorrected verbal fluffs, the sometimes out-of-tune guitar, all seemed the work of a young man impatient to be done and move on. The mood was infectious, but I had two more years of high school, so had to live out the urge to leave home by taking Saturday trips alone to New York.

Nevertheless, when school resumed, I enjoyed my classes. I fulfilled my final science requirement with chemistry, and for the first time in a science course got good grades. There was something logical about concepts of valences and bonding, and fascinating about the awareness that everything from asteroids to the cells of our body was composed of the elements depicted in orderly rows on the chart on my wall. It simply made sense, all a matter of mathematical calculation. I learned to use a slide rule, but also learned to avoid simple mistakes by working out in my head first where the answer should be on an order of ten. This trick was a legacy of Charlie's drilling at the supper table, as he posed challenges based on Trachtenberg's speed mathematics. I also took my last math class, Algebra II. Our advanced placement history class took an issues-oriented approach, reading excerpts from primary sources on various sides of questions of past days and debating them. I did well in classroom discussions but grew dissatisfied over the course of the year. It seemed as if none of these old controversies had ever been resolved; they just died out, and public attention turned to other topics.

In English class, also advanced placement, our teacher,

a hawk-beaked aesthete, seemed amused by class discussions. At one point he interjected an observation. It was surprising, he said, how much better I was orally than in my written work. What would have happened if I had taken this as an invitation to a follow-up conference with him? Could we have explored together why this was so? Could he have passed on practical tips of the craft of writing, as Charlie had shown me how to make good coffee? Perhaps this would have spared me years of missed deadlines, poor grades, and occasional sleepless nights. The teacher also made no secret of the fact that he didn't agree with some of the required books on the reading list, especially O. E. Rolvaag's immigrant prairie saga, *Giants in the Earth*, which a class wit renamed *Clods in the Sod*. Many of the other assigned books—*The Scarlet Letter*, for instance—, were much better, though I only discovered this decades later when I finally read them. My avid reading continued, but so did my aversion to required reading. There were exceptions, such as *The Return of the Native*, my introduction to Thomas Hardy. I also enjoyed poetry and plays, not only reading all the required Shakespeare texts, *Romeo and Juliet* in the tenth grade, *Macbeth* in the eleventh, and *Hamlet* in twelfth, but reading others in summer vacations, both great ones like *The Tempest* and no-so-great like *Timon of Athens*. I enjoyed taking roles whenever scenes were read aloud, especially if they called for mimicking dialects, such as the Norwegian immigrant father in *I Remember Mama*. By this time editions of George Bernard Shaw and Eugene O'Neill offered by the Book-of-the-Month Club adorned my shelf, and I read my way through most of both sets. I supplemented the Livre de Poche edition of Rimbaud's poems found at a *buchiniste* in Paris with a bi-lingual edition of his *Illuminations* from the bookstore in town, where I also bought Woody Guthrie's *Bound for Glory*.

Field trips were always welcome breaks in the routine: *Romeo and Juliet* at the McCarter Theater in Princeton, a trip Off-Broadway to see *The Fantasticks*, or a matinee of Puccini's *La fanciulla del West* at the old Met, soon displaced by the Lincoln Center. Our French class went to an art-house cinema in New York to see *Les parapluies de Cherbourg*. It may have been on that trip, or one of my solo trips, that I found a store specializing in foreign language records, and bought a Françoise Hardy LP, she too dressed in an appropriate fashion in a black turtleneck in the cover photo. Her songs helped me learn idiomatic French expressions more pleasantly than by studying, and my French test results exceeded the amount of time I spent preparing. In general, I had more interesting things to do than homework, and this was the year it caught up with me; in my senior year, I was no longer placed in A. P. English or history.

It didn't help my schoolwork that I had become aware of an additional teaching of the people behind *The Plain*

Truth. It had been evident that they saw adherence to the Ten Commandments as a solution to many of the social ills they decried in their articles. This assertion seemed self-evident, given my Lutheran upbringing, and may have been why I delayed writing to request a booklet they offered on the topic. Booklet offers were part of their strategy, in addition to providing free subscriptions to the magazine. At the end of many articles, there was a reference to a free booklet for further reading. I didn't realize it at the time, but with every request, one took a step on the path toward commitment. Nor did I know yet what that commitment would mean.

When the booklet on the Ten Commandments arrived, I was surprised to find that I had never been taught what the fourth commandment meant. I could recite it from memory, "Remember the Sabbath-day to keep it holy," but had never been aware of the implication, assuming we observed it every Sunday. Now I learned that the Sabbath was the day celebrated by the Jews. Perhaps I should have known this. The closest house of worship to our house was Temple Emanu-El, a Reform synagogue, and on Saturday afternoon cars that overflowed its parking lot lined our street. On the other hand, many of the other stores in town had Jewish owners, and most of them didn't close on Saturday (I also made more than one ham sandwich for the store-keepers in the delicatessen).

Nevertheless, I incorporated this new understanding into my life, in my way. When homework was assigned on Fridays, I knew I wouldn't do it; I left my schoolbooks in my locker when I went home for the weekend. Looking back, I don't know why I didn't think I could do my homework on Sunday afternoon, nor did this new piety prevent me from going to dances or parties on Friday evening or to football games on Saturday afternoon.

To supplement reading *The Plain Truth*, I listened as often as I could to its companion radio program, *The World Tomorrow*. When I sought it out after seeing it advertised in the magazine, I discovered that I had already often fallen asleep to it on my transistor radio under the covers at night, since it followed broadcasts of Mets' baseball games on WJRZ. The main speaker was Garner Ted Armstrong, son of *Plain Truth* editor Herbert W. Armstrong, who spoke once a week, on Sunday. It came on just as the family arrived at Tante Mudel's house for lunch after church services; I often stayed in the car to listen while the rest of the family went inside. The first marks I made in the Bible given me for my confirmation were during one of these Sunday noontime programs. Armstrong's topic was to argue that the Ten Commandments were in force in the New Testament. As he went from point to point, I took out a pencil and marked a Roman numeral for the appropriate commandment in the margin next to each passage to which he referred. I wasn't sure if it was all right to mark a Bible, but I wanted to be able to look at these passages again.

The fact that the older Armstrong had a clearly-defined topic made his programs (I only learned later that these were re-runs of old broadcasts) noticeably different from those of his son, whose livelier approach was more free-form. Otherwise, their approach was similar, as was the sound of their voices.

There were times I resisted their growing pull. At one point, I resolved to stop reading the magazines and listening to the broadcasts. Within days some unsettling news about atomic arsenals reminded me that the Armstrongs had not invented the H-bomb, that our world was threatened with self-inflicted annihilation, so I resumed reading. It wasn't long before Barry McGuire took similar apocalyptic pronouncements to the top of the charts with "Eve of Destruction." Like the Ramona addressed in one of Dylan's songs, I was being fooled into thinking that the finishing end was at hand. But *The Plain Truth* was not only purveying a message of doom; its article stressed that this was only a phase presaging the return of Christ to usher in a bright future, the Millennium. Anxiety coupled with the confidence that it was all in God's hand; everything would turn out right in the end.

In February 1965, the magazine updated its appearance, running a full-color cover for the first time, and changing the frame around it from salmon to pale blue. Cover boy was Winston Churchill, who had suffered a stroke as the magazine was going to press, and had died by the time the magazine arrived. His state funeral had a different feel than that of President Kennedy fourteen months earlier. I had watched the earlier one in a daze, with the poignancy of unfulfilled hopes and the shock of a violent act adding emotion. This one had been unexpected for another reason, as if you expect people who were fixtures in public life to always be there, even if, at ninety, they were no longer active. Even more than at the time of General MacArthur's death the previous April, there was the feel of the passing of an era. Churchill had been the symbol of stubborn resistance in the most hopeless days early in World War II, when it seemed as if Hitler's juggernaut was unstoppable. In their praise of him, the editors of *The Plain Truth* were, on one level, sharing in the general esteem most in the English-speaking world felt toward this hero, yet on another, giving the event a characteristic twist, reminding readers of Hitler's incomprehensible decision not to annihilate the defeated British, French, and Belgian forces trapped on the Channel coast. Churchill himself called their unexpected, successful evacuation a "miracle of deliverance." The editors concurred; God had steered the course of events, allowing the Allies to win the war for the one purpose of allowing their magazine to deliver a divine warning before Armageddon and the return of Jesus Christ. In this way, the magazine simultaneously tapped into mainstream feelings and subverted them. Other articles pursued a similar strategy, taking up topics that were subjects of anxiety, approaching them in a manner akin to that of any conservative political commentator, then reaching an impasse, depicting the problem as insoluble, before expressing the conviction that there was no cause to fear, God had the matter in hand and would soon intervene and usher in the "wonderful world tomorrow," their characteristic expression for the millennial rule of Christ from the book of Revelation. How soon they expected this was expressed in the title of another of their booklets, *1975 in Prophecy*.

Even though their predictions proved to be false, there were some lasting benefits from my reading. I had started experimenting with cigarettes in the previous year. Then a new issue of *The Plain Truth* arrived, with an article by Garner Ted Armstrong labeling smoking a sin. Of course, the Bible was written long before John Rolfe brought tobacco from the Jamestown colony to the court of England, so smoking is not mentioned, but the reasoning of the article was convincing: since tobacco is an addiction, it violates, in principle, the commandment against coveting. While I still experimented a little, I was convinced, and soon stopped altogether. Later on, when a friend complained that food didn't taste quite as good to him since he had taken up smoking, I was confirmed in my choice, since I enjoyed eating. One night at a party, fascinated by my friend Tom's pipe, I tried it. The next day I learned that a pipe directs the smoke farther back in the palate, to the spot that stung in pain when the vinegar in the ketchup on my hamburger hit it. So that wasn't for me, either. A side benefit was that this averted another potential point of conflict with Charlie. He and his brothers were ardent anti-smokers, perhaps in reaction to their father and his cigars.

An additional incentive not to take up smoking was my interest in sports. In soccer I hoped to move from the junior varsity to the main squad and succeeded, but not in the way I had wanted. The coach was more impressed with my enthusiasm than my skill and offered me the job of manager. During the week I practiced with the squad, but when Friday afternoon came, and the team played a match against other schools, I was next to the coach on the bench. In addition to having buckets of water ready for half-time and keeping the score sheet, it was my duty to let him know when five minutes remained in the game, in case he wanted to make any last-minute substitutions. After the game, I gathered the sweaty uniforms to stuff into a laundry bag. I had one other duty: in the evening I called the sports desk of two area newspapers and reported the highlights of the game. I was surprised when the season was over to receive a check from each, the first money I ever earned as a journalist. I had been their stringer without knowing it.

That was the year I joined my first band as well. Graduates of our school, whom I had heard play many times at dances at school and the local YMCA, had renamed themselves from the Vibratones to the more British-invasion-sounding Critters, and had released their first single. Their success set off a flurry of band formation. I joined one organized by Steve, another denizen of the folk club at school, and bought a guitar from him for $75, one-third down, the rest paid in weekly $5 installments. It was a Guild solid-body; the electronics were primitive, but the action was excellent. I was a bit of an outsider in the group; they were all good friends, I was merely an acquaintance. Their taste in repertoire was a bit too much top-forty for me, and their real interest was jazz, something I knew nothing about. I tried to remedy this by borrowing a multi-disk compilation from the local library. It introduced me to some of the older players, King Oliver and such, but the dim sound of these well-scratched sides didn't reach me as Harry Smith's *Anthology* had. I drifted out of the group after a couple of months, then posted an ad at the local music store, offering my services as a vocalist-guitarist, but didn't hear anything for a few weeks. I continued writing my poetry and songs but remained shy about showing them to others.

I had also begun giving guitar lessons. I had not had formal lessons, my music-reading skills were rudimentary, but those were not disadvantages. The classmates who came to me for lessons wanted to learn to accompany themselves on folk songs. I knew the difficulties of the usual approach, which began in the key of C. That works fine on the piano, no sharps or flats to confuse you; applied to the guitar, it's not long before you have to form an F chord, not easy for a beginner. My experience had taught me that the most accessible key to start with was D. That chord, plus the G and the A7, were the easiest to play. With those three chords, you were up and running, ready to play two-thirds of the songs my students wanted to play. Throw in an E minor, also easily done, and you've added another ten per cent to your repertoire. This approach worked—there were quick results, so there was positive reinforcement for the learners. As the weeks went on, I showed some simple bass runs to move from one chord to another. Then I introduced the capo, since you don't want to sing every song in D, added the C and A minor chords, which, together with the 7 variant of the D chord, meant they could play in G as well as D. New students came by word of mouth, I didn't charge much, but what I earned was a good supplement to my allowance, enabling me to pay off the electric guitar.

The students were all girls, which added to the attraction. One of them, Kathy, was cute and I developed a crush, which didn't lead to anything, but she recommended me for guitar lessons to the best friend of her older sister. The friend, Mary, was tall and slim, had a good singing voice, and wanted to learn the guitar. Our lessons started but soon led to something more.

After a few guitar lessons, Mary and I began harmonizing on some songs. She was a fan of Ian and Sylvia, so together we learned their arrangements of "Swing Down Chariot," "Captain Woodstock's Courtship," and many more songs from their repertoire. We added a few songs from the Weavers and my collection of back issues of Sing Out!. Soon we were demonstrating our skills to family and friends, then to the school's folk club, which had an open-mike at its monthly meetings. And it wasn't long before she became my first serious girl. Her family had moved from Virginia a few years before. She was gentle and well-mannered, loved off-color jokes, smoked and wore a perfume called April Violets.

I had a low self-image, and couldn't believe that such an attractive girl liked me. On top of that, she was a year ahead of me at school, meaning that others might have thought that she was dating someone beneath her. We enjoyed the many afternoons we spent together, but I was convinced she was not in love with me, rather a projection of her invention, something I didn't want to disturb by bringing up my increasing interest in the Christian faith as interpreted by this obscure publishing house in California. When it did slip out once, she told me that her older brother, also named Henry, had subscribed to *The Plain Truth* in the past and had been very enthusiastic for a while. I sensed treacherous shoals; I didn't want her to tell me why her brother had stopped reading the magazine. This was important to me, and I didn't want anyone talking me out of it.

Dylan released his fifth LP that spring, his best to date, *Bringing It All Back Home*. On one side, he even used electric accompaniment; although spare, it was still enough to inflame further part of his fans, those who still saw him as flag-bearer for their favorite causes. But others, including me, thought he was getting better at doing what he did best, with the visionary lyrics of "Mr. Tambourine Man" as his best song yet. I heard it on the radio before the LP arrived in the local store, and on first listen misheard "evenin's empire" as "England's empire," making me wonder if Dylan too knew of the hidden identity of the lost ten tribes, as propagated by *The Plain Truth*. Many of his earlier fans thought he had now abandoned protest songs, but to me, there was plenty of protest, especially in two successive songs on the flip side, "Gates of Eden" and "It's All Right, Ma (I'm Only Bleeding)." The final track, "It's All Over Now,

Baby Blue" had, like "Restless Farewell" on his third LP, a valedictory feel. On the surface, it was simply a break-up song at the end of a relationship, yet there also seemed to be a message to his fans.

In that late winter, early spring 1965, Dylan began inching toward widespread acceptance. The strongest track on his newest LP was released with a jangling electric 12-string guitar accompaniment by the Byrds, often cited as the beginning of the amalgam called folk-rock. The ribbing I took from my classmates increased; they repeatedly conceded that some of Dylan's songs might be all right, but only when others sang them.

In addition to the music I heard on recordings and the radio, and that which Mary and I played, I also began to listen to live music. The National Honor Society at my school put on a concert in late winter each year. In 1965, they invited Judy Collins, accompanied by Eric Weissberg on second guitar and banjo. She was the other big female name on the folk music circuit, and aficionados argued over her merits compared to those of Joan Baez. It was like Coke and Pepsi; you couldn't be for both. This strife seemed ridiculous; I thought each was good in her way. And for all the disadvantages women faced in those days, they had one advantage: they could sing well and look attractive, yet still appeal to the folk crowd.

That spring Mary and I went to a blues workshop in

New York organized by Dave Van Ronk, suitably gruff and scruffy. He performed a few songs, explained a few things, but mostly showcased two rediscoveries, Mississippi John Hurt and Skip James. They both wore suits, but no one suspected them of not being authentic. The tracks they had recorded during the Depression were legendary; then they had disappeared from view. I sketched all three on my program using Mary's eyeliner, and Mary urged me to go forward after the workshop to show them. Van Ronk was very approachable; I shyly showed him, saying, "I think it looks like you." "I'm afraid it does," he roared back. He introduced us to Hurt and James. The contrast couldn't have been stronger: John Hurt was the gentlest soul imaginable, while Skip James was frightening. Yet they both had made indelible music. I should have learned that day that you didn't have to project an image, but be who you were and make the best music you could, but that would take a while to sink in.

Easter approached, time for a family visit to Georgia. I had changed in the two years since our last visit, and so had the South. Or rather, it was under pressure to change and was resisting as much as it could. I had no clear view and was torn. Two summers earlier, I had watched the march on Washington and had been riveted by Martin Luther King, Jr.'s, "I have a dream" speech. Yet I vaguely felt that people of color had their "place," and was frightened by the violence that had erupted near our town the following summer. Much of the music I listened to and liked was either performed by blacks or influenced by them. The closest I had been to color-blind had been as a baseball fan—Henry Aaron and Willie Mays were clearly equal to Mickey Mantle and Stan Musial. The story of Jackie Robinson's courage and controlled fury stirred me. A worker at our store had pitched in semi-pro ball as a young man; I pumped him for his memories of facing Josh Gibson and others who never had the chance to demonstrate on a level playing field that they were as good as Babe Ruth and other national stars, perhaps even the best ever. Margie's family was implacable, though. Their opinions of blacks and their experiences with them reinforced each other in a vicious cycle. At best, they were viewed as childlike, at worst, as a threat that had to be kept strictly under control. Also, my instincts were wrong and led to awkward moments. One time I arrived at a doorway simultaneously with a woman who did a bit of housekeeping for Granny. My training said "ladies first," hers was not to go through before a white, even a gangly youth such as I. Neither moved; I felt my discomfort and hers.

Half of my heritage was from the South, but it was turning out to be as much a source of inner conflict as the German half. Our biannual trips had made the way of life congenial, from grits and sausage with fried eggs in the morning through the fried chicken and biscuits with sweet iced tea for supper to falling asleep at night to the rumbling of hundred-car long freight trains. Granny lived in a small town out in the country. When it was first incorporated, around the turn of the century, it quickly boomed. A rail line passed through the heart of it, there were two stores, one of which housed the post office. My great-grandfather, whose grandfather had first settled there soon after the Creeks and Cherokees had been encouraged to sell out and move, was one of those fabled many-hat personalities down south: storekeeper, station-master, postmaster, and justice of the peace. Cotton was king and times were good. Then the boll weevil arrived. The bust was as rapid as the boom had been. The feeling of downward mobility added to the lingering psychological impact of the devastating loss in the Civil War.

The town was situated half-way between two county seats. Each featured as its main attraction a memorial to the fallen sons of the Confederacy. Granny and her sister regaled me with tales of their father—the snowy-bearded prophecy buff—and his time in the war, including the time General Lee visited their unit, and they urged him back; it was too close to the front lines. His wife was from Atlanta, and her younger sister entered history as the first civilian casualty when Sherman attacked. I still have the tintype photo of her in her coffin.

At the same time, the memory of Dr. King's speech and the emotions of the many songs of the civil rights movement drew me in the other direction. I sensed that one of the girls in German class was sweet on me. Like me, she was half-German. But unlike me, her mother was German, and her father, who had met her mother as a G. I. in Germany, was black. Even though I thought she was nice, I never acted on the impulse to ask her out. I didn't want to experience Margie's expected reaction. Of course, she changed, too, in the course of her long life. She was over eighty when I coaxed all I could out of a faded wedding picture of the parents of my great-grandfather. It had been taken in 1866. The bride was a war widow, the groom was back from the war, in which he had fought together with two of his brothers, one of whom died in battle. He was the next-to-the-youngest of fourteen children of his father, a man who had been among the first settlers in the area, but died long before his younger children were grown, leaving them orphans. Those who were still minors were separated, taken in by various families in the area. His bride carries a look of sadness, he of stoic resignation. There was something else that intrigued me about the photo, something elusive in the faded image. She was appropriately pale, his skin seemed nut-brown by contrast. Of course, women were expected to avoid sunlight to keep their skin pale, whereas he had undoubtedly spent much more time outdoors—day and night—in the previous four years than indoors. But combined with his wavy hair, I couldn't help but speculate. When I gave the restored photo to my mother, for which I had found an imitation-wood oval frame, I asked her cautiously whether he didn't look a little "Spanish," an old euphemism she immediately understood. Her answer gave me insight in how far she, too, had traveled in her long journey: "It wouldn't matter if he were."

Fooled into Thinking

Chapter Five

We returned from Georgia on my seventeenth birthday but took a detour before heading home to stop at the motor vehicles office in Plainfield so that I could get my driver's license on the first day possible.

Charlie had been fascinated by motors since he was a little child, even before his brother Herman had come back from America with the first automobile in their village as a present for their parents' silver wedding anniversary. Charlie, twelve-years-old, looked after it, kept it running, and drove it over the backroads, although he could hardly peer over the dashboard. The local constable was sure he was doing it, and was on the lookout to catch him, but never did.

I wasn't as fascinated with cars as Charlie had been, but was eager for mobility and all it portended. It didn't bother me that to Charlie it meant someone who could run errands, picking up equipment and parts throughout Union,

Essex, and Somerset Counties when I went back to work at the store in the summer after my junior year of high school.

First, you learn to turn over in your crib. Then you painstakingly figure out how to crawl; I loved to crawl and reluctantly left it behind in exchange for the greater range and speed of mobility on two feet. Each stage was a further step in deciding where you wanted to go, which is one way of deciding who you want to be.

Now, as a teenager, my life was once again going through stages that led to more mobility, thus more independence, and perhaps, increased self-determination. My driver's license sped me along on the path that had begun when I spent the previous summer away from home and was, in turn, a transition before leaving home to go to college. That destination was still vague, but I was impatient to go. Holding a driver's wheel in my hands enabled me to widen my radius while I waited for the next sixteen months to pass.

On a practical level, having a driver's license, and the use of Margie's white Buick Special station wagon made it easier to transport my burgundy Guild guitar, amp, and home-made microphone stand, as well. By this time I was in a band again, this one fronted by Michael Fennelly, an excellent guitarist and vocalist who had been in other bands around town. Mike had written a few songs, including two that would form the heart of the set-list for this new band, and wanted to do something more than top-forty covers. I sang a couple of my songs when I auditioned, and Mike saw the possibility of writing together.

For the drummer, I recommended Alan, a boy from my homeroom, an introvert with eyes of watchful suspicion known at school for his bursts of speed through the hallways. He was a misfit, was Maynard G. Krebs to my Dobie Gillis. A bad knee had put an end to his hopes of excelling in track, so he devoted himself to a drum kit. He provided a solid rhythm, although his knee acted up at times, lending some unpredictability to the bass drum; that and his sardonic humor helped keep us loose. Mike's neighborhood friend Dennis played harmonica and added background vocals. We advertised for a bassist and added Chris, who split his loyalty between ours and another band. Good bassists were in short supply.

By the summer we were ready to appear in public, starting at a backyard pool party in Mike's neighborhood. This occasion was not, however, my first time on stage with Michael. That had happened a couple of years before, in junior high school. I was walking down the hall after school one day in ninth grade when some pupils burst out of the auditorium. When they saw me, they asked: "You sing, don't you? Do you know 'Tom Dooly' and 'Mr. Blue'? We need you!"

There was to be a music assembly that Friday, and Michael, then an eighth-grader, had organized the group. He was to sing and play guitar; the others were to add harmony. Now he had been caught in some infraction, and the punishment was not to participate in the show. So I was drafted to replace him.

Friday came, the principal relented, and Michael could perform. Since I had rehearsed with the others during the week, though, I went on as well. Mike's backing trio had become a quartet.

Now, for our new band, most of the repertoire came from Mike, both his compositions, and songs he suggested. Alongside a few tunes each from the Beatles and the Stones, we looked farther afield for the rest of our material. Three tracks from the first LP by the Pretty Things, with a cover photo making them look grittier even than the Stones, which for us meant closer to the real thing, supplemented by "I Love the Way You Walk," a reworking of a John Lee Hooker song, a little-known track by P. F. Sloan, "The Sins of the Family," and three songs by the Beau Brummels, who had had one big hit as a West Coast answer to the British invasion, after which each successive single landed progressively lower on the charts, despite in our opinion getting stronger and stronger. Mike's after-school job at the town record store afforded him access to an endless number of possible tracks. I often stopped by on my way home and listened to Mike's latest discovery in one of the two booths. Our special love was for the Zombies, adding the B-sides of their hits to the growing set. Nor were we averse to improvising; at one dance the following winter we spontaneously launched into an extended jam on the theme song from Davy Crockett, with a Dylanesque refrain, "King of the wild fronti-uhh!"

One contribution to our shared taste came from me, though. In October 1965 I urged Mike to go with me to Carnegie Hall to see Bob Dylan in concert. Our seats weren't bad; we were about twenty-five rows back, a bit right of center. The first half was an entirely acoustic set and included some tracks from his recently released *Highway 61 Revisited*, including a memorable rendition of "Desolation Row." I was in awe of Dylan's ability to sing all the lyrics from memory; there were no on-stage teleprompters in those days. And that song to me was part of the continuing refutation of the charge that he had somehow abandoned protest music. No, this was more radical in its protest than his earlier songs.

After an intermission, Dylan came out through the curtains for the second half, still with an acoustic guitar strapped on. He threw off the opening riff of "I Don't Believe You," then stopped and said "It used to go like that, now it goes like this," at which point The Hawks, as they were still called, broke into the new, electrified version, as the curtains parted. It was compelling showmanship. You

103

can hear the routine on his release of the show a half-year later at the Manchester Free Trade Hall in England, a show long-bootlegged as the Royal Albert Hall concert. But by that time, the introduction was stale, the joke was flat, and it was no longer used as a curtain-opener.

When I first heard the bootleg of that show in the early seventies, I recognized the arrangements as those I had heard, but they were played with a different spirit. In Carnegie Hall, there had been none of the invective with which he spits out the lyrics to taunt the crowd in Manchester, nor an enraged crowd reaction, with the famous shout of "Judas" clearly heard. No, in New York he had sung with conviction and fire, but was on his home turf, with a hall full of people who were prepared to follow him in the jingle-jangle evening.

When the entire Manchester concert was issued as volume four of Dylan's "Bootleg Series." I was surprised to hear the first, acoustic half, dismayed at the way Dylan tossed off these songs as if he couldn't be done with them soon enough. In New York, the first half had been just as heartfelt and convincing as the second. But the impatience that had driven Dylan since he first came east from Minnesota as a college dropout continued to fuel him and led him from one creative peak to another, or so it seemed at the time. A wheel on fire, rolling down the road, but—as it turned out—one shortly to explode.

After seeing Dylan and the Hawks at Carnegie Hall, there were memorable concerts on a near-monthly basis. In November, Alan, Mike and I went to the Mosque Theater in Newark, or as it was recently renamed, Symphony Hall. We had seats in the last row to see the Rolling Stones, waiting impatiently while listening to the opening set by Patti LaBelle and the Bluebells. After an intermission, the Stones came out for a twelve-song set, opened with "Everybody Needs Somebody to Love." We were enthralled from start to finish, even when Keith Richards' lead cable went bad during his riff for "Satisfaction," a mishap that set Charlie Watts laughing on his drum stool as Ian Stewart scurried out from the wings with a replacement.

A month later I returned to Symphony Hall to see Pete Seeger. While tamer than the previous two concerts, Seeger had no equal in his unassuming, unforced gift for getting an entire auditorium of people to sing with him. Seeger was no stranger to the building, either, commuting down from his self-built cabin on the banks of the Hudson to do a weekly television show, *The Rainbow Quest*, in a studio upstairs. The show appeared on one of the new UHF channels breaking up the stranglehold that the three dominant networks had on the VHF band. Of course, the New York metropolitan area had already been better-served than many areas, being a market large enough to support stations on all seven possible VHF bands. In addition to flagship stations of each network, there were three independents and one outlet for the fledging public television. But there was a hunger for more, so stations such as WNJU Channel 47, with studios above Symphony Hall, rushed to fill the airwaves. We would soon be inside those studios.

How this immersion in the flourishing music world could be reconciled with the doomsday visions that filled the pages of *The Plain Truth* was a question I pushed to the back recesses of my mind. At times, there was a close correspondence; P. F. Sloan seemed to be cribbing a *World Tomorrow* radio script when he wrote "The Eve of Destruction." At other times, the two clashed, as when a *Plain Truth* article decried the youth culture, illustrating it with a photo of the five members of the Byrds, taken just after they arrived in London on their first transatlantic flight, eight miles high.

I was careful to conceal my slowly-coalescing convictions from my bandmates. One day at practice, Mike recounted watching *Elmer Gantry* on television the night before, then launched into an impromptu revival sermon. I responded by flopping onto my knees and offering a mock testimony. In my mind, this was no contradiction. The figure Sinclair Lewis created, a religious huckster who preyed on gullible parishioners, was surely not a true Christian, not to be compared to Herbert W. Armstrong, who I felt was on the level.

Meanwhile, tension was rising at home over my continued reading of *The Plain Truth*. The December issue contained an article about Christmas, "The Greatest Story Never Told," pointing out differences between what people commonly believed about the holiday and what the Gospels recorded. It went on to allege that the choice of December 25 was a tie to pagan celebrations as the days finally stopped growing shorter, and the sun had been reborn. I didn't keep this new-found knowledge to myself, and as I worked side-by-side with Charlie in the days leading up to it, preparing many trays of party sandwiches in his store, I made my feelings known. Christmas had been Charlie's favorite day his entire life. Born at the beginning of December, he had been named Klaus for St. Nicholas (Charlie was his Americanized name) and christened in church services on Christmas day. Although the gifts in his childhood were meager—highlights being a fresh orange and marzipan—it was the high point of the year. This was still the case for him as an adult. December 25 was the only day in the year the store closed, but leading up to it, he put in extra hours, after closing-time, designing and building a winter scene for the window display, then, as the day drew closer, fulfilling lucrative orders for holiday food. His few hours home offered enjoyment as well: buying, setting up a fragrant pine tree, having the children fetch decorations from the attic, and stretching strings of colored lights through the evergreen shrubs outside. The family gathered around the piano from year to year on Christmas Eve to sing the traditional songs, then, almost too excited to sleep, the children were shepherded to bed so the presents could be pulled out of hiding to be ready when they crawled back out of bed at first light. A greeting card idyll that I would likely have sought to destroy from adolescent perversity alone, but now with the added resolve of religious conviction. I didn't want any presents, I said, but was delighted when I received them nonetheless: two new turtlenecks and new LPs. I got the Byrds' *Turn, Turn, Turn* and the second album of the Beau Brummels, my brother, the Beatles' *Rubber Soul*. We took turns playing them on our parents' stereo in the living room while getting ready to leave for church, I reluctantly, with a grimace worthy of a Grinch throughout the morning, deepening to a condemnatory scowl by late afternoon as we headed to Uncle Herman's house for the family party. The next day I was back to work in the store, working side-by-side with my hurt father. It was a relief for both when vacation drew to a close after New Year's, and I headed back to school.

The band continued rehearsing, although our disdain of a hit-dominated playlist didn't lead to many appearances. One day a classmate who organized the dances at the YMCA sneered, "You guys think you're so hot. You need to hear the band from the shore I just booked." So Mike and I were front and center studying licks when the Castiles, Bruce Springsteen's high school group, played. Yes, they were good, but so were we, we felt. Convincing others was the challenge. Somehow we landed on the bill when a promoter was looking for local bands to open for Tony Orlando, whose last hits on the chart were a few years back. Unfortunately, I was in bed with a fever and a throat infection. Doctor's orders: I was not to go on stage. Charlie would have gone to work if he had been as sick. It didn't seem fair that I would be deprived of the chance. I did insist at least on attending, despite my family's objection. I have no clear memory of the show. Mike's recollection is that it was canceled at the last minute.

On another occasion, Mike and I brought our electric guitars and amplifiers to folk club one day to perform a couple of blues numbers, with Alan filling in on his melodica. Afterward, we stored the equipment in my car, but when school let out that afternoon, found that the gear had been stolen. I drove to the delicatessen and told Charlie, who told his friend, a detective on the town's police force, and that evening we had our instruments. The detective had a hunch who might have done it and went to where he lived before he had a chance to fence the equipment. Sometimes I didn't mind that Charlie was a lifetime member of the Patrolman's Benevolent Association.

Despite the lack of playing in public, when Alan urged

us to take a shot at playing on television, we felt we were ready. The show, *Disc-O-Teen*, appeared every afternoon on WNJU and was hosted by Zacherle, who scored a hit a few years earlier with Boris Karloff-imitation novelty records such as "Dinner with Drac," but was better known for his comedic interruptions of the horror films he hosted on TV. *Disc-O-Teen* was similar in format to Dick Clark's long-running *American Bandstand*, with local teens dancing to hit records and guests stopping by to promote their latest singles, with one difference: each day, a local group played a live, three-song set as part of a competition for a record contract. We applied, but to my dismay, our appearance was slotted during spring vacation. Although we had been to Georgia the year before, we planned to go back again that year, given Granny's declining health (she died a year later). Although Charlie was less than thrilled by the time I put into band practices, time he would rather I had spent on homework, he understood that it was important to me, so he agreed to allow me to fly to Georgia the day after our TV appearance.

We arrived for the pre-show set-up and sound check. Once the amplifier volume had been set and the microphones placed, we were solemnly forbidden to touch anything. That made sense, but one of us made a smart remark, to which the sound technician self-importantly informed the group that he knew what he was talking about, he had engineered a hit single for Reparata and the Delrons. That was all we needed—we had somehow landed in *Hard Day's Night*, and we knew from then on how to play the roles. Next was a briefing from the producer, whose attempt to gain our cooperation ended with saying "I wrote Soupy Sales," which I supplemented, not missing a beat, with ". . . Fan mail." There was an additional cause for the pre-show nerves of the staff: The Duprees, a doo-wop group from Jersey City who, with many others, had been knocked off the charts by the British invasion, were scheduled as in-studio guests, but were late. In fact, they never showed, and when it was time for their slot, Zacherle pulled us in front of the camera, and we instantly became Alan, Dennis, Chris, Mike, and Henry Dupree. The host conducted a not-quite straight-faced interview, and we responded in kind, then lip-synched with exaggerated gestures the new single, having never heard it.

Oh, and we played our three-song set and didn't do badly. We finished second in that week's voting, a result that disappointed a little, but we felt richer for the experience.

The next day I took my first flight to join the family for our vacation in Georgia, what was to be my last time there. Two flights, to be precise; the first on Eastern Airlines from Newark to Atlanta, from where I took a cramped propeller plane for the bumpy trip to Macon. Dazedly looking around for my connection in Atlanta, I nearly knocked over a man who turned out to be a country singer I recognized from television.

The tensions of a northern boy and his southern relations hadn't lessened in the interval since our last visit. Margie's Uncle Hal took exception to my hair; Charlie tried to protect both himself and me by explaining he usually would not have allowed it to get that long, but let it pass because of the upcoming television appearance. Well that was past now, so Uncle Hal took me to his barber at the county seat. He went on some errands; I waited for him on the sidewalk after the cut. He returned, wasn't satisfied with the results, and marched me back to the barber's chair for a second round. Or at least that's how my sister Edith told it in later years, and she generally had a good memory. I have no recollection of it; that's what is called suppression.

I had a guitar with me. In order not to disturb the others, I played mostly outdoors, but that led to a worse disturbance when a black youth, attracted by the sound, approached the house and we started talking. I was reprimanded for encouraging that kind of contact.

This trip was the last time I saw my Georgia relations. When I had been younger, I had a particular liking for Uncle Hal, whose given name was Henry, with his hunting dogs and back-pocket flask. His tobacco-rasped voice and

112

soft Georgia accent were well-adapted for the stories with which he entertained my siblings and me. I liked his wife, too, Aunt Caroline, a willowy redhead whose wily charm and steel will made her the epitome of a southern lady. But as the song says, the times they were a-changin', and I was now separated from them not only by a generation gap but also by a clash of cultures, and I was on their home turf. I regretted that my last visit to Georgia was clouded in this way. I had enjoyed the trips, and this was part of my heritage.

Not only my family, but the whole country was riven. The civil rights movement was one factor, the growing involvement in Vietnam another. The summer before entering high school Jeff, John and I not only trained for football, we shared a fascination with guerilla tactics, hiking the nearby Watchung Mountains, reconnoitering. If the Russians invaded, we wanted to be ready to take to the hills, knowing the terrain. John flew missions in Vietnam, becoming a Lieutenant Commander in the Navy. Jeff joined the Marines right after high school graduation and was in Vietnam within weeks.

On my seventeenth birthday, I acquired the right to carry a driver's license in my wallet. On my eighteenth, the obligation to carry a draft card.

There was no immediate danger of going over. Like most of my classmates, I had applied for and been accepted to college, after being in a quandary about it throughout high school. Some of my friends seemed to know exactly where they wanted to go and what they wanted to study. One was accepted by Harvard, another by Princeton, others to some of the elite smaller Ivy League schools. Marc, who had given me my first Dylan record, went to Antioch, in keeping with his politics. Frequent articles in *The Plain Truth* praised the virtues of a college affiliated with that magazine, Ambassador College, where neatly-groomed grounds and stately buildings (per the prose descriptions, accompanied by panoramic photos) provided an environment to cultivate values as well as learning. At a loss to know where I might want to study, I wrote a letter expressing my interest. Margie revealed years later that a "college representative" (in truth it was a minister) had telephoned the house, but I wasn't home, and she told the caller I was no longer interested. Charlie reasoned with me: "California is a long way off, and no one has ever heard of this small college. You have no basis for comparison. If you consent to attend a college closer to home for a year, then I won't object to a transfer."

I had no idea how to compare schools, no strategy for applying. My male cousins had gone to Lehigh, but they had studied engineering or accounting. Although I wasn't sure what I wanted to do with my life, those two choices were low on the list. If I had chosen in junior high school, it would have been for a school with a strong history department, but that had receded. I was interested in media, whether writing for print, radio, or television, and wanted to continue to make music. A friend recommended Lafayette, Lehigh's rival, just across the Delaware River from New Jersey; from there I could commute back to appear with the band (as Jimmy Ryan was doing from Villanova with the Critters). The two of us drove there for a Saturday orientation for applicants. We attended a class, and an English professor had us to his home with other applicants for a chat, a setting straight out of *The Halls of Ivy*, a television show from the fifties. In the course of the day, I discovered that all freshman were required to take the geology class we had attended, on Saturdays. Perhaps a subtle way of keeping observant Jews from applying. I had already applied, and went on to be accepted, but had already promised myself I would get serious about Sabbath observance when I got away from home, so my choice fell on the other school to which I had applied, Boston University. It was a strong contrast to Lafayette. No well-defined, secluded campus, with a small number of students, but a string of buildings, some of them high-rise, strung along busy Commonwealth Avenue. Charlie and I drove up to look it over shortly after we returned from Georgia. Not knowing any better, we went on April 19, an ordinary day throughout the country, but in Boston, it was celebrated as Patriot's Day in commemoration of the outbreak of the American Revolution. No university offices open, no classes to attend. We did get into one of the dorms and talked to an upperclassman, a resident assistant for his floor of the dorm. As we sat in his dorm room, walls adorned with *Playboy* pin-ups, he did a good job selling us on the virtues of the school. I was ready to be sold. I liked the idea of living in a city, but perhaps not one quite as large as New York City. I knew there was an active coffee house scene, which I was eager to join. And although it was a large university, it had a small School of Public Communication, which offered recognized programs both in broadcasting and journalism. Best of all, there were no required Saturday classes. There was a significant proportion of Jewish students, even higher than I had known in the advanced placement classes in high school, so I would feel at home.

After the experience of going steady the year before, my social life in my senior year was more varied. Mary had left for college in Kentucky; we broke up during the summer before she left. For a while, I dated a girl who lived on the same street as she, Carolyn. We had met in French class, and I liked her personality, a mix of fun-loving and seriousness. Her passion at the time was surfing. I gave it a try but never mastered it. We dated, but there was no spark; we were meant to be friends, nothing more. Toward the end of the summer, when she started dating

Mike, there were no hard feelings; it seemed a natural development, and they were a pair throughout that school year. Meanwhile, I brought a different girl each week to weekend parties, drive-in movies, or concerts and club dates in New York. A compulsive list-maker, I started one of the girls I had kissed. After a late start at sixteen, the list grew long before I left for college. For a while, I was sweet on a quiet, dark-haired girl I got to know in the creative writing club but was competing for her affections with the son of the owner of a clothing store in town. In addition to the mystique of going to a private school, his strategy included discrediting me by putting down Dylan. His cousin had been claiming for the past three years that Dylan had bought "Blowin' in the Wind" from him. Coming on top of Paul Clayton's bad feelings over the guitar pattern used in "Don't Think Twice", and Dylan's use of Van Ronk's "House of the Rising Sun," this seemed credible. On the other hand, I asked myself, what has that guy written since? Dylan's creativity, meanwhile, seemed to be accelerating. Only years later did the true story come out. The cousin had spotted the song when *Sing Out!* published it, before Dylan recorded it, learned it, and indirectly passed it off as his own. When it became well-known, he was too embarrassed to admit he had been misleading everyone.

My senior year of high school passed quickly, yet not fast enough; I was impatient to leave. I would come home after soccer practice, drink a quart of milk but eat very little, lie down for a nap, then use any excuse to go out in the evening. Studying at the library was an ever-acceptable alibi, but sometimes I met others at a pizzeria instead. Once, without telling our parents, Mike and I drove to Plainfield to answer an ad in the local newspaper. A man had ambitions to become the east coast Berry Gordy and was auditioning local talent. We hadn't brought any equipment, but I sat at the piano in the back room of a bar and chorded one of Mike's compositions while he sang. It went over well but didn't lead to anything.

Another welcome reason to go out were meetings of the Explorers, the wing of Boy Scouts for older boys. I had enjoyed donning the blue uniform of a cub scout in elementary school, and with sporadic effort had earned a modicum of badges. I continued to Boy Scouts in junior high, but my only memento is a photo of me in me green uniform standing uncomfortably next to Claudia, the girl I took on my first date, a dance put on by the troop. Mike had continued to the next level, but the local post risked disbanding because of dwindling numbers, so he recruited Alan and me. The three of us were able to set the tone at the weekly meetings. We also went for two weekend camping expeditions that fall and winter. I stopped at the store after school Friday afternoon before the first of them. Charlie took a rum cake out of the display case, went next door to Uncle George's liquor store for a bottle of rum, and soaked the cake with it (the rum flavor used in baking was non-alcoholic). The cake was a hit the next evening. The second trip was my introduction to spelunking. We explored a cave in Pennsylvania, just beyond Virginville, rich in stalactites and stalagmites. At one point, the passage we had to take was partially filled with water. To get through, we had to press hands and feet against the two side walls. It was exhilarating to be challenged in this way and to find that I could do things I wouldn't have expected myself to be able to do. At the furthest point inside, we turned off our lanterns to experience darkness in a way I never had before. Normally it is never so dark that you have no sense of dimension, but here, without light, the world ended directly in front of my eyes.

Another exercise in self-reliance came one afternoon when the brakes failed in my car. When I first got my driver's license, I used Margie's white Buick station wagon. This had been useful in carrying band equipment from our practice room, which was first in Mike's basement, then Alan's, to our gigs, or transporting Carolyn and her surfboard to the shore. But in the fall of my senior year, my parents bought me my first car, a green, four-door 1948 Dodge, as old as I. They bought it from one of Charlie's customers, a widow who had been the only owner. She rarely drove it but had dutifully vacuumed it every week. I invest-

119

ed in new tires, gaskets and hoses, the bill totaled more than the car purchase, and for the first few months, I had to break it in almost like a new car. One day I was in Plainfield on an errand for Charlie, and noticed, while parking, that I had no brakes. Since I was just rolling slowly at the time, it came to a stop when the tires bumped against the curb, but how was I to get home? I called Charlie, who expressed confidence that I could get the car home, instructing me how to use the gear shift in combination with the handbrake to negotiate any eventuality. After completing the five-mile trip, I felt good about myself, and also about Charlie for believing I could do it.

I had been dropped from advanced placement classes in history and English. After the free classroom discussions in the tenth and eleventh grades, it was a challenge to adjust to more normal instruction. When the class read *Hamlet*, and the protagonist tells Ophelia to get to a nunnery, I suggested that this was a euphemism for a brothel. Years later, I found some scholars had proposed this understanding, but at the time, the color drained from our teacher's face. It was more extreme in history class; I clashed with the teacher, sometimes heatedly. It proved easy to make him livid by suggesting that Karl Marx may have had a good idea or two. But he was fair-minded enough to allow me to take part in the highlight of the year in class, when we held mock elections, recreating the

1912 presidential election, the election that had brought the Bull Moose candidate to Westfield. The teacher taught several sections, and in each that day, three students gave speeches they prepared presenting the platforms of the three candidates, Woodrow Wilson, Teddy Roosevelt, and the incumbent, William Howard Taft. The coveted role was that of T. R., Teddy Roosevelt, but in my section, that went to another pupil. I reluctantly accepted Wilson, but then threw myself into preparation. Charlie drove me one evening to the P. M. Bookshop in Plainfield, and we came home with a stack of books, historians' accounts as well as reminiscences by Wilson aides. It was fascinating reading, and in the course of it, I began to see how I could counter the speech I expected from "T. R." (I wasn't worried about Taft). I also decided to play the local card, since Wilson had been governor of New Jersey at the time he ran for the White House. The morning of the speeches, I rose early, as I liked to do when I had to make a presentation, and immersed myself in the topic. I didn't write out a speech but spoke directly to the class based on an outline in my head. Our section met in the last period of the day and was the only one in which Roosevelt didn't win the mock election, but Wilson. This was one of my first experiences of speaking to a group, and I liked it.

The disappointment of being dropped from advanced placement sections was balanced by winning a slot on the yearbook staff. The staff had its own homeroom, so for the first time I was not with many of the same pupils I had been with since the seventh grade (normally homeroom assignments were alphabetical); instead, I was grouped together with others who shared an interest in good writing and publishing, many of whom I knew well from the A.P. classes I had been in. Having our own homeroom, with the yearbook advisor as homeroom teacher, meant that we could use the last period of the school day, and beyond, to work on it.

I eagerly joined in the team process of photo selection and copy-writing. One memorable afternoon, Ken, another of the staff members, rushed in. He was also president of the folk club and involved in arranging that year's National Honor Society concert. Now, on this Wednesday before the weekend of the concert, the promoters told him that Ian & Sylvia, who had been booked, had canceled. Among the replacements they offered was Donovan. I had been in New York ten days before, when the British singer had debuted in Carnegie Hall, and urged Ken to accept. At the concert, the sounds of dismayed teachers and parents sucking in their breath when he took the stage in tight slacks, a satin jacket and topped with an unruly mass of curls was almost as enjoyable as the music. Although the yearbook was nearly ready to go to the printers, the staff decided to devote a page to the evening, something that had not been done for Leon Bibb or Judy Collins in the previous years. I didn't take time to consider what this signified about the increased acknowledgment of pop music; I was busy selecting the photos, writing captions and copy, and laying out the page, which had been entrusted to me.

More practical publishing experience came when another staff member, Alan, who was also literary editor of the Writers' Club, called on my aid to finish compiling their magazine, which contained my first published poems.

It was also time for standardized tests: National Merit Scholarship, college boards, and the scholastic aptitude tests that would influence acceptance to the college. We had taken PSATs, preliminary tests, the year before; now we took the full version. Our guidance counselors encouraged us to sign up for as many advanced placement and achievement tests as we could fit in. I took an A. P. exam in history, and achievement exams in German and French, scoring well on all three. In history, I scored a "1" (the highest grade) in the question-and-answer portion, but only a "2" on the essay. My factual knowledge was evidently stronger than my ability to analyze, reason, and construct an essay, but the combined result was good enough that Boston University granted six credits for U.S. history alongside freeing me of language requirements.

Graduation approached. Despite treating homework as an afterthought, the average of my grades put me on the borderline to be included in the honor group, designated by a different color tassel on the pasteboard cap that went with the gown, but it didn't happen. I heard some talk that the decision had more to do with the length of my hair (not quite long enough to be sent home) and my habit of wearing blue jeans to school, which until then had not been tolerated. I didn't know if there was any truth to the rumor; based on the amount of work I had put in, I didn't deserve any honors (there had also been rumors I was getting the French award). But the suspicion that the reason might be my freewheeling image, rather than my academic performance, flattered me.

Meanwhile, Alan's status was also shaky, but for another reason. He learned after final exams that he would not graduate. He appealed, and the administration allowed him to repeat his U.S. history exam. If he passed that, he could graduate. He and I spent a day together in his room, and I gave him a crash course. I assumed Alan knew more than he thought he did, so I devoted my efforts to helping him get a framework in mind for what he knew. I started by pulling out a dollar bill and explaining why George Washington's picture was on it. To me, the last five letters of the word "history" told it all: it was a story, one as intriguing in its way as any spy thriller or science fiction work. Classroom instruction seemed oriented toward dates, treaties, and names that could only be digested if one knew the plot. The cram session paid off; Alan graduated with me and five hundred and fifty others that June 22. A chapter in our shared lives closed, and we were eager to see what the future would bring.

The words on the opening spread of our yearbook express the feelings we had: "We hold in our hands the kaleidoscope of the future . . . with limitless vision . . . with power of truth and knowledge . . . we will have the ability to change the patterns of the world . . ." Perhaps common sentiments for high school seniors, but we were just starting to sense what it meant to be at the heart of the postwar baby boom. Those born in the U.S. in the late forties may have been the most privileged generation ever to live. Yes, perhaps we would change the patterns of the world.

By this time I knew that I would leave for Boston in ten weeks. The School of Public Communication sent two books to read over the summer, C. P. Snow's *Two Cultures* and Alfred North Whitehead's *The Aims of Education*; I supplemented this by working my way through Marshall McLuhan's *Understanding Media*.

In the meantime, I would work another summer in Charlie's store, the third time I would spend my summer this way. Charlie decided to use my help to tackle a big project. The store had its own well, and it was time to pull up the pipes, check for damage, clean out rust, and put them back down. He could have hired a well-digging company, but that was not his way. He maintained the heating and air-conditioning for the entire building and repaired all of the machinery. Some felt he should spend more time in the store, waiting on customers. He knew he could hire good, hard-working people to work the counter, and he hated spending the money they took in on things he could do himself. I suspected an additional reason: the routine of store-keeping was not enough for his active mind and powerful body. So we constructed a tall tripod from which to suspend a winch and chain, and we started to work. Section by section we hauled the pipe up, taking each off with a pipe wrench and knocking it with a sledgehammer to loosen rust. Slowly a stack of pipes grew to the side of the hole until we had all 150 feet of pipe out. Then the process was reversed, with careful attention to the threading, which we coated with plumber's gook before reattaching each piece and lowering it down. I enjoyed working side by side with Charlie, and to be Charlie's legs to fetch any tool he needed. One evening after the work had gone especially well, as we sat down for supper, Charlie passed me a beer, telling me, "you worked like a man today, you can drink like one."

He was preparing us both for my departure. At the beginning of the summer, he told me I had no curfew. It would be my decision when I came in each night, as long as I spent each night in my bed and was on time for work each morning. Charlie's reasoning was that come fall he and Margie would have no idea of what I was up to, so this was a step on the way.

Charlie also understood that I had no interest in furnishing my college wardrobe from the ivy-league oriented clothing stores in town. On a day off we drove to a youth-oriented store in lower Manhattan, where I bought a three-piece suit with four buttons on the jacket (that fourth button was a symbol of non-conformity) and a sport jacket with an oversized glen plaid pattern and epaulettes.

One stifling summer day, with 100 per cent humidity and temperature over 100 degrees Fahrenheit, when opening the door to go out felt like entering a blast furnace, I used my work-break to venture out to go down the street to the Music Staff to buy Dylan's newest, *Blonde on Blonde*. I brought it back to the delicatessen and waited impatiently for closing time, took it home, and put it on. A double-LP, with an out-of-focus portrait on the cover, and some long songs inside. One filled an entire side. There were no timings listed, so I counted the revolutions of the turntable as it played, and divided the result by 33⅓, and arrived at an astounding 12 minutes and 34 seconds. While the calculation was a little off, it was still a long song, longer than any before on a pop record. But the length by itself would have been meaningless if it hadn't served the hypnotic power of the song, "Sad-Eyed Lady of the Lowlands." There were others that impressed me, "Visions of Johanna" for one, a song I began teaching myself that same evening, and others that confused me by their off-handedness, such as "Rainy Day Women #12 & 35" and "Leopard-Skin Pillbox Hat." The sparse liner notes revealed he had not recorded this in New York, as he had all records until then, but in Nashville. Yet this didn't sound like country music. He seemed to continue an astounding arc of growth. A few days later, the news spread that Dylan had suffered an accident on his motorcycle. Just months earlier, in April, I had gone to the bookstore and was the first to buy Richard Fariña's *Been Down So Long, It Looks Like Up to Me*, only later learning that he had been killed that day when he wrecked his motorcycle after the launch party. This was an eerie parallel, but Dylan had not been killed, or at least, no death was announced.

While waiting in vain for news of his condition, I continued to listen in amazed enjoyment to the music issued that summer both in recordings, such as new releases by the Beatles and the Rolling Stones, but also live at the Gaslight in Greenwich Village or a number of open-air concerts at the Wollman Skating Rink in Central Park. I even drove to the Newport Folk Festival. Charlie consented to let me go for one evening, on the condition that I show up for work on time the next morning. So with Nan, the girl I saw that summer, I drove up in time to catch the evening concert, with Judy Collins, Phil Ochs, and Buffy Sainte-Marie. I made it to work the next morning and somehow dragged through the day.

My musical tastes were not limited to what was now being called folk-rock. Rummaging through the over-stuffed hall closet, I found a set of 78 rpm records with the Chopin *Preludes*, until then unknown to me. I played them repeatedly, especially on rainy days mirroring the Paris print on my basement wall, and even worked out a passable arrangement by ear of the one in C minor on my guitar. Flipping through a bin of marked-down reel-to-reel tapes at the local hi-fi store, I came home with Beethoven's *Eroica* conducted by Adrian Boult. Bored with the predictability of the three top-forty radio stations from New York, I scanned the dial for alternatives, often landing at Newark's WNJR, especially enjoying their evening DJ, Rosko; other times I pulled in WWVA, Wheeling, West Virginia, through the late night static to hear hillbilly music. And I had continued in the Glee Club at school. We had a new director in my senior year who supplemented a basic repertoire of Fred Waring arrangements with adventurous material by Vincent Persichetti, Alan Hovhaness, as well as my favorite, Randall Thompson's setting of the last words of David. Another strand was woven in when I met a new boy at school from India. Spurred by the sitar I had seen Sean Philips use accompanying Donovan in a concert, I asked about Indian music. It turned out that his mother played the sitar, and I took a few lessons, starting with what was to me an exotic way of counting time.

Friction grew in the band over the summer, hardly unusual in a group of adolescent boys with varying degrees of talent, ambition, and maturity. It reached the point where I quit. After a couple of weeks had gone by, we were surprised by a phone call from WNJU. It was time for run-offs in their contest, but one of the five bands that had qualified had disbanded in the meantime. Would we be interested? Whether the show's producer remembered us because of the quality of our play, or because of our smart-mouthed wit, it didn't matter. A face-saving way was found for me to rejoin the band, and we prepared for our second appearance on *Disc-O-Teen*.

The afternoon didn't start auspiciously; I drove to Mike's house to pick him up for the drive to Newark, but he wasn't there. A frantic search through the neighborhood located him splashing in a neighbor's pool. Was it his way of dealing with pre-performance nerves? We quickly loaded our equipment, drove to Symphony Hall, and went upstairs to the studio; by this time my head vibrated to the beat of a headache. The performance went well, though, and we were voted the best of the five groups to play that week, winning the right to compete in the finals.

We also heard of the chance to audition at the Night

Owl, a club in Greenwich Village where the Lovin' Spoonful, Tim Hardin and others had gotten their start. We drove in one hot afternoon, auditioned, and received a positive judgment. We were still a little raw, had to strengthen the list a bit, according to the club manager, but he liked our original material and talked about the possibility of a weekly slot after we had a bit more polish.

With these prospects, I proposed coming back weekly from Boston on Eastern Airlines, which had recently introduced a relatively inexpensive shuttle service. Dennis was leaving for college in California, but there seemed no reason we couldn't continue as a quartet. One day toward the end of summer I brought my Wollensak reel-to-reel tape recorder to Alan's basement for rehearsal. I plugged Mike's microphone directly into one track and recorded the rest with a microphone aimed at the speakers of our amps. It was a primitive set-up, but the result wasn't bad, and my intention was to use this to rehearse on my own in Boston while the others practiced in N. J.

As the day to leave for Boston approached, I was in good spirits. I had long been eager to move out and make my own decisions. This didn't mean I was quite ready to become what is sometimes called a self-directed person. I hoped to get away from three roles I felt I was playing, or three sets of expectations I felt pressured to live up to. There was what parents, other relatives, and teachers expected. The generation that had fought World War II had returned to build a prosperous and powerful society of which they were proud. I just had to conform, make a few compromises, and I could have my part of the American dream. Then there was the persona I projected to my friends. We saw the hypocrisy in the picture our parents offered and decried the injustices that fueled it. Although we gleefully shared in consumer goods generated by the muscular economy, we had our own style: not Brooks Brothers, but blue jeans. We were just as conformist in our non-conformism as our parents but were convinced we were individuals, more authentic. And there was a third pull: the person I felt I should be as a Christian in the interpretation of the group in California that published *The Plain Truth*. Despite the reproduction of Rembrandt's "Peter's Denial of Christ" in view whenever I sat in my basement refuge, I was embarrassed to let this side show in the town in which I had grown up. My hope was that in the anonymity of a big city campus, I could live the life I felt called to lead.

By this time I had become aware that there was a church behind *The Plain Truth* and Ambassador College. Perhaps I could begin attending services? The idea of transferring to Ambassador after a year remained in the back of my head; one reason for my choice of communications as a course of study was that I could perhaps be useful in helping produce the magazine, the radio program, or their fledgling television program. Articles in *The Plain Truth* promoting Ambassador—they were frequent—warned against coming there with the idea of becoming a minister; that was a calling, not a profession one chose. That was all right with me, I had no desire to be a minister. In fact, I had an aversion to the possibility ever since I was pulled to the side by an inebriated uncle—the one all the cousins avoided at family parties as the evening wore on—who told me I should become a minister, because then I could have all the women and money I would want. So no, not a minister. But I had bought into the idea that there were only a few years left to communicate the truth and wanted to help in that.

Who was I as I bought my clothing, packed my suitcases, and completed my summer reading? Who was the person at the center of this triangle of expectations? It is not unusual for a young person to search for a sense of identity. At the time I didn't realize that identity is not a thing, a constant, something independent of outside influences. Nor was the solution to my quandary the total embrace of one or the other of those three personae, though at the time, my intention was alignment with *The Plain Truth* corner of the triangle. It took me a long time, far beyond the time covered in this book, to learn that identity is dynamic, and can only be realized in relation to others, and that all three of these poles were sources for the network that is identity. I was pulled in these three directions because all three were part of who I was.

Chapter Six

It was early on a September morning, before sunup, when Margie, Charlie and I loaded Charlie's capacious white Buick Elektra for the drive to Boston. We made rapid time, and were the first ones in the room I was assigned to share on the fourth floor of a nine-story dorm on Bay State Road, Myles Standish Hall (since renamed Shelton Hall). In its previous incarnation as the Sheraton Hotel, it entered literary history; Eugene O'Neill had died just thirteen years earlier in the room two doors down from mine.

The "rooms" had been designed as three-room suites. The original bedroom of the suite was considerably larger than the other two rooms and had only one bed. There were two beds set in the central room, and another bed in the room to the other side of the suite. First one to arrive, I took the larger room and began unpacking my books and clothes. Pride of place went to two high school graduation presents: a manual Olympia portable typewriter—a marvel of German engineering—and a blue-bound Webster's *New Collegiate Dictionary*. Both received intensive use in my four years in Boston and beyond. If the value of a gift is measured not in its purchase price, but in the place it takes in the life of the one who receives it, then they were two of the most valuable gifts I ever received.

I found the thought of city life exhilarating, but Margie saw only the soot on the windows; she sat on the edge of the bed and began to cry. The dirty windows crystallized all that she didn't want to happen on that day, to leave her oldest child in a strange city five hours from home. We couldn't change that, so we did what we could. We went to a grocery store down the block, bought a bottle of Windex and a roll of paper towels, and set to work cleaning the windows. Soon my roommates arrived, and my parents left. The moment I had been anticipating for years was here. I was on my own. I hung my Rembrandt print of Peter denying Christ over my desk. Now I no longer needed to put on another face but could act on my desire to live a Christian life, as defined by the writers of *The Plain Truth*.

My roommates were personable, and we hit it off well. Tom came from Shillington, Pennsylvania, John Updike's hometown. Bill was from New York City and had spent the summer as a bicycle courier, fearlessly negotiating the city streets. Rounding out the quartet was Mark, a tall, athletic local boy.

My resolve to be a Christian mixed with my eagerness to explore the folk scene. A day or two after arriving, I bought a current issue of the Boston version of *Broadside* magazine, and learned of a weekly open mike at the Unicorn Coffee House, hosted by a DJ whose voice was already familiar to me from WBZ, a strong-signal Boston station I had pulled in at home in New Jersey. I slipped my pawnshop guitar into the canvas cover Margie had sewn from a pattern Pete Seeger had printed in *Sing Out!*, designed so that you could attach the guitar strap on the outside and carry the guitar on your back, and walked to Boylston Street, placed my name on the list, took my turn, and sang my songs. It was my first time on stage in Boston, in one of the clubs long known to me only by name.

I chatted a bit with some of the other hopeful musicians. One of them, Paula, was also there for orientation week at B. U. She had enrolled as a drama major at the School of Fine Arts (SFA), but sang as well. Her main inspiration was Odetta, who had heard her sing once and encouraged her.

I ran into Paula again a day or two later; she was headed for Harvard Square, together with two other SFA first-year students. Would I like to come along? So the four of us crossed the river. In the course of the next few hours, my attention increasingly focused on one, and the other two slipped away unnoticed, leaving us alone on the roof of the

Coop, Harvard's student store, with a panoramic view of the Square and of Harvard Yard. She was Sian, and from that afternoon we were inseparable for the next two-and-a-half years. She was the one who knew that secret passageway off an alley on Palmer Street to the fire escape that led to the roof. Life was not going to be as straightforward as I pictured it after all.

The secret passage was only the first of many things she showed me in the days to come. She was a local girl, but that week marked the first time in her life she had been in a public educational institution, having been schooled exclusively in convent schools, first in one near her home in Brookline run by French nuns, then high school in another, less-expensive one, involving a long commute. She was musical, having studied piano for eight years, and was enrolled as a voice major.

Sian was a little less than medium height, and wore her dark hair long, parted in the middle, accentuating a widow's peak. Together with her dark eyes, set against her pale skin, and her aquiline nose, her look was arresting, reminiscent of Joan Baez, but with a much fuller figure. Our conversation deepened with the shadows of the fall afternoon, flitting effortlessly from music to movies we liked to glimpses of the life each had lived until then. She knew her way around the Square and enjoyed showing me many of her favorite nooks and crannies. Then we walked across the Boston University Bridge, through the west end of Boston to her family's apartment.

An only child, she lived there with her parents. Her father came from a large Boston Irish-Catholic family; her mother was from Nova Scotia, an Anglican who had consented to have her child raised Roman Catholic as the condition of marriage, as was the norm in those days. Both worked and were out much of the time; even when her parents were home, we were left to ourselves. We talked deep into our first night, saw each other the next day, and the day after that. Late that night, just before it was time for me to go, she took my hand and placed it on her ample, soft breast, through the thin nightgown she had changed into, as if to say, this is yours for the taking. After spending my senior year in high school with a social life that avoided entangling alliances, I found myself in my first week in Boston in my second serious relationship, this one even more so than the first.

True to my resolve, I made no secret of my interest in God and the Bible, but this was not a negative in her eyes. Although she no longer wanted to be restricted by all that the nuns considered right and wrong, she had an abiding, genuine interest in religion. Though our views often coincided, they also conflicted in ways that would cause us both heartache in the coming years.

Meanwhile, the semester was gearing up, and it was

time to register for classes. For Sian, there were not many choices; music students had full days, and most of their courses were directly related to their major. For those in the School of Public Communication (SPC), it was another matter. In the first four semesters, we took one core course per semester in one of the four areas of concentration at the school. For the rest of our load, we were encouraged to take a broad range of courses at the College of Liberal Arts (CLA). I signed up for required two-semester courses in Western Civilization and English composition and rounded out my program with geography, sociology, and economics.

In those days the idea of studying journalism in college was not widely accepted; Harvard, for instance, offered not a single class in it. It was far from the only school not to. Of the few colleges that offered a degree in media, some offered a highly-professionalized program, an environment that simulated the working world students would encounter after graduation. SPC pursued a middle course, reasoning that while it was important to prepare for a career, it was also necessary to have a good general education to cover news competently.

In the bracing fall air of a university environment, I resolved to put my dilettantism behind me and become a good student. That resolve conflicted with the fact that most of the time Sian and I were not in class we spent together. I often waited for her toward the end of her instruction- and rehearsal-packed days at the SFA building, a no-frills converted auto showroom. I spent so much time there that some of the others began to ask what instrument I studied. When I replied that I was waiting for a friend, they expressed their envy: "You're lucky—you can enjoy music!" Sian and I studied side by side and often interrupted each other. We sometimes met at the library, but more often we worked at her apartment. More than once I stayed after the last streetcar back to the dorm had left, and walked home in the middle of the night. There were films to see on the weekends, and folk clubs to visit. I continued auditioning and singing at open mikes, but the two of us also worked up some arrangements in which she sang to my guitar accompaniment, leading to a regular booking for her at one of the clubs. We let that lapse after a few months after getting the impression that the club owner appreciated more about her than her voice.

Another damper on my scholastic enthusiasm was the way in which classes at the university seemed a step backward compared to those in high school. Then, I had compensated my lack of diligence in homework through active involvement in classroom discussion. It was a major channel for learning, as well as the primary way to show I had learned something, all appearances to the contrary. Now most courses were taught as lectures in a large auditorium, and few by gifted lecturers. Sian enthused about one of hers, Joel Sheveloff, who lectured on music history; I sat in a few times, concurred, and looked forward to the humorous anecdotes she shared after the classes I didn't attend. My classes that year were lackluster by comparison. The one exception was an introductory film course, one of the SPC core requirements. The professor, Tony Hodgkinson, was English, claimed to know Marshall McLuhan, but didn't take it badly when I disagreed with some of his interpretations of *Understanding Media*, which I had read over the summer. He showed us documentaries from the Canadian National Film Board, had us analyze David Lean's *Great Expectations*, and assigned other weekly papers. We formed two-person teams to make 8 mm films; I made mine together with Len, an aspiring sports broadcaster from Fitchburg. In it, the protagonist wanted to sit in the park and read the Bible but, ashamed to be spotted doing so, hid it between the pages of a *Playboy*.

Professor Hodgkinson's favorable comments on my weekly essays contrasted sharply with the reactions from my English teacher to the writing assignments and required journal entries. When I reread the English journal years later, I found my memory had magnified her criticism, and minimized the quality of the writing. While some entries were embarrassingly bad and some of her assessments drastic, over the course of the year, my writing improved, and her comments became guardedly encouraging. There are those who claim that good writing can't be taught. That's not entirely true; I learned much from reading and rereading Strunk and White, as well as from the critiques of friends over the years, but in the end, you learn to write by writing. What redeemed the class for me at the time was that, although a CLA course, our section was composed entirely of SPC students. My roommate Len was in it, as well others I knew from our film class. I got to know Andrew, who became a lifelong friend, in that class.

Not only my resolve to be a diligent scholar, but also my plans to commute back home for gigs with the band never materialized. A month after I left for Boston, Mike dropped out of high school to hitchhike across the country with Alan. After arriving in Los Angeles, he spent a few days with Dennis at his college, then gravitated to the Sunset Strip, arriving just in time for the youth protests immortalized in Stephen Stills's song, "For What It's Worth." Mike slept at first on the floor of one of the clubs at the center of the protests, wrote a song about it and was filmed singing it for the evening news. Alan was not as enamored with California and soon hitchhiked back home, staying only a week in New Jersey before showing up in Boston, where he remained for a few days in a rooming house not far from my dorm before his restless spirit led him back to New Jersey.

It wasn't long before Alan returned to Boston, though, this time as road manager for a group, Thorinshield. When the musicians arrived, I agreed to meet him at the radio station where they were due to be interviewed. Alan never showed, but I enjoyed chatting with the group as the DJ sent out fruitless calls over the air for Alan Action, as they called him.

While my studies were characterized by bursts of enthusiasm alternating with periods of distraction and neglect, I did have the self-discipline to begin each day working for a half-hour on a Bible correspondence course from Ambassador College. I was an early riser, usually up long before my roommates, and enjoyed this peaceful time. The course was elementary. Each lesson was devoted to a topic; after introductory comments, there were a series of questions, each to be answered by writing out passages from the Bible. It was teaching by rote, by indoctrination, based on a literalistic view of scripture. Humans have questions, and the Bible has the answers; all that was necessary was to locate the proof texts.

The course didn't encourage theological thought, but the discipline of looking up verses and copying them in long-hand did help me find my way around the vast collection of writings contained in the Bible and gave me my first acquaintance with many passages. I ordered more booklets from Pasadena, and by springtime wrote to request my first visit from a minister of the Worldwide Church of God, the church behind *The Plain Truth* and Ambassador College.

In the meantime, my growing interest and commitment led to conflict with Sian. At first open to many of the things I shared with her, her resistance grew whenever they clashed too greatly with her convent-school training.

The worst strife came when I received a book by Garner Ted Armstrong, *The Plain Truth about Child-Rearing.* Her father lapsed periodically in his struggle against alcoholism, and she and her mother suffered violence when he came home morose and full of self-loathing after one of his sprees. When she read of Armstrong's prescription of corporal punishment, beginning at a very young age, she couldn't help but view it in light of her experience and react strongly. At the time I thought this book, like all the writings from Pasadena, contained the gospel truth. It took me years to see that of all the literature produced by the church, this book was the most damaging. There were many families associated with the church who instinctively provided a loving environment for their children, who didn't turn out badly despite the spankings they received. Other families failed to do this. Mechanically applying the teachings of this book in unadulterated form, they broke the spirit of their children.

Many of these children are now middle-aged and still coping with the effects of this worst sort of behaviorism.

We had already talked about a shared future. Beyond the question of how to raise children, were we to have any, was another issue: in which faith would they be raised? One of the rhetorical tropes employed by the Worldwide Church of God in its literature was expressed by the question, "Where is the church that Jesus founded?" This question arose from words attributed to Jesus in the Gospel according to Matthew, "I will build my church." Writers in *The Plain Truth* made much of the singular form of the noun, contrasting it with the hundreds of denominations in America. At the time, I didn't notice the sleight-of-hand in calling denominations "churches" and shared in the conclusion that this was a self-evident contradiction of what Jesus said he would build. Growing up Lutheran, one of the main celebrations each year was October 31, the anniversary of Luther's legendary nailing of his 95 Theses on the door of the castle church at Wittenberg. I had loved the evening service held to commemorate it, joyfully singing "A Mighty Fortress Is Our God." Now, Luther's break with the Roman Catholic Church had become proof that the movement that grew out of the Reformation could not be the original church. Sian agreed: there was one true church, and it was either the church of Rome, with all its faults, or this tiny, unknown group in Califor-

146

nia. We reached a compromise. She had no objection to my receiving a visit from one of their ministers if I would consent to meet with a priest. I had already gone with her to a Saturday night social at the Newman House on campus, a forlorn occasion with undercooked chicken. Nevertheless, I agreed to talk with the campus priest, a Paulist Father.

For me, the deciding factor between the truth of the claim of the Roman Catholic Church to be the one true church and the competing claim of the Worldwide Church of God was the question of the Sabbath. Did the command to rest on the seventh day still hold, or had it been abrogated? The Protestant churches often made an appeal to scripture to decide the question, pointing to the conflicts Jesus had with Pharisees when he healed on the Sabbath; I didn't see in them an assault on the Sabbath but as a difference of opinion on what was appropriate activity on the day. God had rested at the close of creation week; to restore the hopelessly broken seemed in keeping with the will behind that creation. More challenging were the appeals to Paul, but his arguments weren't easy to grasp. Sometimes he appeared to be upholding divine law, at other times to say that it was no longer binding. At the time, influenced by *Plain Truth* articles on law and grace, and by the speeches of Paul recorded in the Book of Acts, which portrayed him as observant throughout his life, I was convinced that the Ten Commandments, including the Sabbath command, were required for Christians. At the very least, I concluded, there was no clear statement in the New Testament that the Sabbath was no longer to be kept. It would be decades before I spotted the flaw in this; that discovery led to the dissertation that I eventually wrote as a middle-aged man.

The priest came to my dorm room one spring evening, and we had a pleasant talk. I raised the question of the Sabbath, and was surprised by his calm answer: "We changed it, and we had the right to change it."

So here was a point of agreement between the two churches: the issue was not decided in the New Testament, but was a question of faith and practice outside of its pages. The only question that remained to be decided was whether a church had the authority to change the Sabbath.

By this time I had studied a lengthy booklet by Herman L. Hoeh, *The True History of the True Church*. Unsurprisingly, the question of historical origins would be important in deciding the question I was facing. I didn't know it at the time, but Hoeh availed himself of a trope beloved of non-conformist churches for centuries. In answer to papal charges that the churches of the Reformation were rebellious daughters of the mother church, the dissidents argued that the church of Rome never was the church Jesus founded, but a counterfeit foisted on the world in the murky centuries before Constantine made it the official religion of the empire. At the time I didn't notice the west-

ern bias in both sides of the argument; the Eastern churches were little-known to me then.

Hoeh argued further, as had many writers before him,
that this counterfeit was foretold in scripture. A remarkable feature of the final book of the Bible, Revelation, is
a set of seven letters, written to "the angel" of each of
seven congregations in the Roman province of Asia, today
in western Turkey. They form chapters two and three of
the book and differ in form and content from the chapters
that follow. While addressed to actual congregations of
the time, known to the author, recipient of the visions recorded in the book, the oracular nature of the letters lends
credibility to the assertion that there was a second level of
meaning to them, and that they in some way contained a
message for the church in general at all times (the repeated exhortation in each letter, "He that hath an ear, let him
hear what the Spirit saith to the churches," seems to imply
this). Building on this, Hoeh and those before him pointed
out that these churches are listed in circular order, the order in which they would be visited along a postal route. An
argument flowed from this: that the local congregations
represented successive eras throughout history, from the
first founding in the time of the apostles (represented by
the congregation in Ephesus) to the time of Christ's return
at the end of the age. Three of the letters are positive in
their overall tone. Aside from that to Ephesus, one was

149

the fourth, addressed to Thyatira. In common with previous interpreters, Hoeh applied this to pre-Reformation "reformed" churches, such as the Waldensians. The other positive letter was the sixth, to Philadelphia. Here is where the widest divergence can be found in "histories" of the church based on these letters. Each is written on the assumption that the time in which the author is writing is shortly before the end of the age. Therefore, the Philadelphia "era" must be the group with which the writer is affiliated. Soon to come, however, from the perspective of each writer, is the final degradation just before the end, the time of the lukewarm congregation in Laodicea.

Hoeh's booklet was my first exposure to this reasoning, and it was fascinating to learn of an underground history, parallel to that commonly told, for instance in the Western Civ course I was taking. Alongside the apostolic succession that the bishops of Rome claimed to reach back to Peter, the rock on which Jesus would build his church (the first links of which were shaky), there was another genealogy, a succession based on passing along the "truth." I learned of "heretics" such as John Wycliffe, Peter Waldo, and Jan Hus, figures whose courage inspired me. In many such reconstructions, this succession is generalized as the truth of the gospel that Jesus had preached, but in the particular tradition to which Hoeh was heir, this was more specific: it was the esoteric truth of the Sabbath.

Since this is hard to verify in the historical record, Hoeh and others made an appeal to the argument of silence: since in many periods of history, Sabbatarianism was considered heresy, and heresy in turn punishable by death, those holding to the true faith had to practice it in private. All the more significant, then, the times when hints of Sabbath observance turn up.

One such instance was the Quartodeciman controversy. The name comes from the Latin word for fourteen and refers to the hotly-contested question in the early church of when to commemorate the death and resurrection of Jesus Christ. One side centered the observance on the fourteenth of the first month of the Hebrew calendar, the other early on the following Sunday morning. Common to both was the account in all four gospels that placed the events during a pilgrimage to Jerusalem for the Passover.

In the reconstruction in Hoeh's booklet, those who held to the fourteenth did so because they continued to practice the Passover in the manner and at the time the Jews had done. Crucially, the debate had a geographical component: those who celebrated the observance on the following Sunday included the bishop of Rome, who claimed authority to decide the question, while the Quartodecimans lived mostly in western Asia, the area to which the letters in the second and third chapters of Revelation had been addressed. Further, they based their practice on what they had learned from a bishop who in turn had known the John who authored Revelation, by that time conflated with the John who had been one of the twelve disciples.

I had heard none of it before this, and the story fascinated me. Moreover, it was one that could be confirmed or refuted by a visit to the newly-built Mugar Library on campus, which I took to visiting Saturday mornings. With time, I made my first acquaintance with the multi-volume collection of Ante-Nicene Fathers assembled in English translation by Philip Schaff in the late nineteenth century and located in it the writings cited by Hoeh. I found that Hoeh's quotations were accurate. That was not the same as confirming his interpretation of the question at stake, but I didn't recognize that at the time. For one thing, I didn't ask myself how it could be that Polycarp of Smyrna, representing the "true" church, remained in communion with Anicetus of Rome even after their talks, in which neither was able to persuade the other. Still, the score was Worldwide Church of God 1, Roman Catholic Church 0 in my mind as I waited for a "representative" to contact me.

After that first long, dark, snow-filled Boston winter, I experienced the tentative approach of a New England spring for the first time. Even more than in the past in New Jersey, the first snowfall in November had been magical, as soft flakes danced in the failing light. The amber glow coming up from the street when I turned out the lights had a different quality, as a thin layer of snow covered the usual grime of the city. The charm diminished as we students walked to class along Commonwealth Avenue, with morning rush hour traffic splashing waves of slush, but the experience was renewed with the second and the third snowfall. It was a different matter four months later, as stubborn, ice-encrusted, pebble-peppered heaps lingered. For months I had yearned to go outside without the burden of a Navy-surplus pea coat, heavy boots, and the thick oatmeal-colored scarf Sian had knit. Cold days gradually took on a softness in the air; the ever-lengthening evening twilight lent an unusual color cast to budding trees and flowers.

Finally, on an April evening, the call came. I was in the shower when the phone rang; a roommate answered, then yelled to say it was for me. I stood towel-wrapped and dripping as a man with an English accent said he represented Herbert W. Armstrong and had called because my request had been forwarded to him. We set a time for an evening the following week.

He didn't come alone but was accompanied by a second man. It struck me as strange, especially since the sidekick maintained total silence aside from a greeting at arrival and saying goodbye when they left. Later I read in the Gospels that Jesus sent out his disciples by two, so I guessed it had been all right. With this man silently look-ing on through his glistening gold-rimmed spectacles, the conversation ran between me and the representative, Reg Platt. He seemed relatively content with the amount of church literature I had read and my understanding but then questioned me about my Sabbath observance, which was not rigorous enough by his standards. So he encour-aged me to improve, then he and his sidekick left.

The next few Saturdays were long; I discovered that "rest" could be harder than work. As much as I was de-voted to reading the Bible with the help of church litera-ture, there was a point of diminishing returns after a few hours. While going through the city would have been too "worldly," I was thankful that a walk along the banks of the River Charles was considered "nature," and that it was all right to admire God's creation on the Sabbath. Not being a gifted student of natural science, I had never appreciated nature so much before in my life.

Sian had trouble understanding why I would no longer see her on Friday evening nor Saturday afternoon, as we had spent every weekend together since first meeting in September, except for Thanksgiving weekend and semes-ter break over Christmas, when I had returned to New Jer-sey. But she coped with it as well as she could, and it made our reunions on Saturday evening more special.

One bond between us was our love of music, and we

enjoyed exposing each other to our favorites; I had moved my turntable and LPs to her room. I overcame my aversion to Christmas to share her enjoyment of Joan Baez's new release, *Noël*. In the absence of any news about Dylan, we listened to the seven LPs he had issued, especially *Blonde on Blonde*, still his most recent. In addition to the Beatles, the Lovin' Spoonful, and the Stones, newer music appeared, much of it from the West Coast. Jefferson Airplane's *Surrealistic Pillow* was a particular favorite as spring arrived. We went to see Donovan when he came to Boston. Was it Dylan's silence that finally allowed him to find his voice, his vocabulary? He wove increasingly intricate patterns of words, and his LPs *Sunshine Superman* and *Mellow Yellow* didn't merely "go electric," as so many folkies did after Dylan plugged in at Newport. Instead, his finger-picked acoustic guitar was supplemented by tasteful, jazz-tinged arrangements. It's hard to recall now, but for a brief period between being thrust into a recording studio much too soon and then receding into an addlepated early senescence, he flourished as a musician and writer.

Through Sian, my acquaintance with classical music widened rapidly. There was a generous student discount for subscriptions to concerts at Symphony Hall, where we saw Janet Baker, Andrés Segovia, Julian Bream and others. We went to student and faculty recitals, my first exposure to composers such as Bartók and Britten, whose music was

challenging at first. Given Sian's talent, I derived some satisfaction from the grasp my autodidactic guitar playing
had given me of music theory, and I often helped her with
her harmony and composition assignments. She assiduously practiced on the piano, with a special love of Chopin's
Preludes, as well as singing the material she worked on for
her voice lessons: "Voi che sapeti," "Frühlingsglauben,"
and a Villanelle by Berlioz. She sang in the Women's Chorus; I sometimes sat in on their rehearsals at the end of the
afternoon, and was at every concert, in one of which she
shone as a soloist, dressed in a black suede dress that made
her look like a Minoan priestess. The chorus also sang fre-
quently in worship services, everything from Episcopal to
Unitarian. So, somewhat reluctantly, I was often in church
on a Sunday morning, sitting near the back, feeling like
a secret agent, an observer, not a participant. These were
not "true" churches, and I was impatiently waiting for a
return visit from the Worldwide Church of God minister, in
hopes of an invitation to attend their services.

In addition to sharing music, we shared our reading enthusiasms. She introduced me to books by Dylan
Thomas, J. D. Salinger, and Saint-Exupéry, all new to me. A
bookcase I built for her reflected our mingled lives: It contained, along with her books, some I had bought for her,
and other books she had bought for me. Sian also had more
sophisticated tastes in visual art than I; having grown up

just a streetcar ride away from museums had opened this world to her at an early age. Through Charlie's collection of art books, I was aware of major artists from Leonardo and Rembrandt to Van Gogh and Picasso, now with her at my elbow, I went further into the twentieth century.

In ways I didn't realize at the time, she also sought to remold me into her ideal man. She had pictured herself married to an architect. Wouldn't I rather be one than pursue a career in media? She may have tried to steer me in a different direction because her father had worked for a Boston newspaper. Together we explored examples of the work of Walter Gropius, Le Corbusier, and Eero Saarinen in the Boston area. We went to the Brookline Public Library and returned to her room with arms loaded with picture books of their work and others, such as Mies van der Rohe and Gaudi.

Boston University was large and offered a broad range of programs, but none in pre-architecture. Harvard did, though. Wouldn't I consider transferring there? There would be a bit more prestige for her as well, dating a Harvard man. Just a little more her dream man.

She also planted the idea of my not spending the summer in New Jersey, but of staying in the area, and we picked up information on summer courses at Harvard's information office on the ground floor of the Holyoke Center.

So when spring semester finished at B.U., I made a

short visit home, then returned to spend the summer at Harvard. The courses I took couldn't have been more unlike each other. With an eye to changing my major to pre-architecture, I chose a class in calculus based on a recommendation from an architecture professor at M. I. T. He had seemed skeptical of my plan; generally, they wanted candidates who were stronger in engineering. Then he added: "Of course, it's not absolutely necessary—Saarinen was not a strong engineer." But he continued with an afterthought: "Then again, his buildings already are falling down." So I took calculus and barely passed. Throughout the summer, I performed the operations but never had a clear view of what problems they were meant to solve. I was sure there was a concept called "calculus" that I just wasn't grasping. I continued for a second semester in the fall at B.U., again ending that with a D, which put an end to my dreams of becoming an architect. It was years later, reading a short biography of Newton, that I read an explanation that I could understand. Sure enough, there was a concept behind it and a particular set of problems it addressed. Once again, recourse to the history of a subject was what I needed to open the way in, but one I had failed to find as a nineteen-year-old.

The experience was not wasted, though; even wrong turns are an education. For me, the value was that I've never been afflicted with the wistful feeling "I could have been. . . ." I admire a well-designed building, whether a large public space or a small home, but I know it wasn't a realistic career goal. The M. I. T. professor summed up our conversation: "With your overall intelligence, you can probably become an architect if you want to, but you'd be a middling one at best." Someone graduates at the bottom of the class every year; it's good no client ever wondered if I were that one.

The second class I chose not for utilitarian reasons, but because it sounded interesting. Henry Hatfield, a professor of German literature, offered a seminar that focused on four authors: Rainer Maria Rilke, Hugo von Hofmannsthal, Thomas Mann, and Stefan George. Mann was known to me, but it was my first exposure to the other three. The course had an ambitious reading plan, preferably in German, although I often had an English translation open next to me as I struggled with Mann's dense prose. Hatfield knew how to balance lecture and discussion. A motivated group of students from all over the country took an active part in the seminar on the top floor of the Holyoke Center. The course could be taken either for undergraduate or graduate credit, depending on the enrollment status of each student, so there were some advanced participants. There was even a visiting professor from Germany. In addition to reading the assigned texts themselves, I had to get up to speed quickly on Nietzsche and Freud to understand the wider intellectual framework of these writers. I spent long summer hours stretched on the lawn in Harvard Yard, or leaning with my back against a tree, with a book open in front of me. Alternately, I used the collections of the Widener and Lamont libraries. Lamont, with its arrangements of modular wooden cases in a commodious reading room, was an especially inviting place to read and work on my term paper on Stefan George. For my topic, I took an assertion in Hatfield's introductory text on modern German literature and challenged it. I worked hard on the paper; more than the grade (A-), I was gratified by Hatfield's closing comment: "You are most certainly right." This course was perhaps my first encounter with a great teacher. He had been curious about why I had chosen to take it since I was not a German major. When he learned of my hopes to transfer to Harvard, he offered to write a letter of recommendation.

Early in the summer, Reg Platt called to offer a second visit. He arrived with a different companion, a young minister, also from England. Like the man who accompanied Platt on the first visit, he remained silent throughout. Not silent was Sian, who insisted on sitting in and confidently voiced her criticisms. We told Platt we were engaged, which in an informal way we were; more important to him was my assurance that I had been keeping the Sabbath more seriously since his first visit in the spring. At the close of the conversation, he said I would be welcome to services.

On the following Saturday, a married couple with two boys arrived at the dorm to pick me up and were disconcerted to find Sian there as well, intent on accompanying me. They were momentarily flustered, having been told only to bring me, but when she assured them that she had met the ministers as well, they figured it would be all right. The two of us arranged ourselves in the back seat with one of the two small boys, and we set off for the drive to services in Manchester, New Hampshire, an hour away. The church may have been "worldwide" (it had only recently changed its name from Radio Church of God), but their congregations were few, and widely scattered.

We arrived and found that services were held in the Odd Fellows Hall, a name that seemed appropriate as we entered the auditorium. The people we met were friendly, but shabbily-dressed, and seemed, for the most part, ill-educated. It was nearly time to begin services, so we found seats near the back. A mother sat in front of us with her small children; their frequent squirms were answered with sharp swats. Even though I had accepted what I had read in the book on child rearing, I found this disturbing, but it was more upsetting to Sian for the memories it evoked.

There was a buzz of excitement in the hall. A leading minister, called an "evangelist," was visiting that day. Ray-

mond C. Cole was there to give the sermon; he pastored
congregations in New York and Newark, close to my home,
and oversaw the churches throughout the northeast as
district superintendent. He occasionally contributed articles to *The Plain Truth*, and I was impressed that, on the
occasion of my first service, I would see such a personality. It took a while, however, to hear from him. First, there
were hymns, more like the Baptist hymns I had heard on
visits down south than the Lutheran hymns more familiar to me. Many of the melodies were written by an Armstrong; it turned out that Dwight was Herbert's younger
brother. There was no organ. Again, like Sunday morning
down south, the accompaniment came from an upright
piano in the corner.

After three hymns and a prayer, Platt came to the lectern for what was announced as a sermonette, something
I had never heard of before, although it was clear that the
word must mean a small sermon. "Small" was a relative
term, though; it was certainly shorter than the message
that followed but was longer than sermons I was used to.
Apparently, he had spotted my uninvited fiancée, and he
peppered his message with what seemed to be gratuitous
impromptu anti-Catholic remarks. The discomfort level
rose. There was another hymn, but still no sermon. Instead, Cole was introduced for what were called announce-
ments. Cole spoke of various events in the news, to which

he assigned prophetic significance, and developments in "the Work," which turned out to be the term used for what the Worldwide Church of God was doing. Although he rambled, the tone of these remarks, as well as the lengthy sermon he eventually gave, was on a more refined level than the first message. More than two hours, and many squirms and swats later, a closing hymn and prayer ended the service. Sian and I were eager to leave, began gathering our things, but the sidekick from Platt's first visit tapped me on the shoulder and told me that Mr. Platt wanted to see us in the counseling room. We joined a line and waited for our turn. He may have planned to interrogate me about why I had brought Sian, even though only I had been invited. In those days, the church expected persecution, due to be part of the "Great Tribulation," which at the time they were sure would begin in five years, in 1972. Services were closed to outsiders, the time and location not published; those who were curious were told about the gravity of hearing things they were not spiritually mature enough to understand. If they heard them anyway but failed to act on them, they could be held accountable in the judgment. For this reason, church members and ministers spoke of "dangerous knowledge." This is what I assumed Platt planned to say, but he never got the chance. Not only had Sian been disturbed by what she heard and saw, but I was agitated as well. We were both ready to burst, and our question was urgent: "Where is the love?" Platt mumbled something about how we express love by keeping the commandments, but the conversation had the feel of a stand-off.

Perhaps the question was provoked in part by the fact that this was summer 1967, the media-acclaimed summer of love, the height of Hippiedom, a movement in equal parts non-stop party and spiritual yearning. But even without this, it was clear that a vital aspect of what we read in the Bible was missing. The protagonist of the Bible, God, is spoken of with many attributes, but only once does it say what he is: love. While it was impressive that the congregation, in addition to being multi-racial, was multi-generational, more so than most worship services we had attended, the display in the row in front of us, as well as the steady stream of parents with a child in tow for a short visit to the "family room," the room that after services became the counseling room, had seemed hard to reconcile with that definition of God, as was much of what we heard from the lectern.

The interview ended, with both Platt and I convinced that maybe I wasn't quite ready to attend services. That might well have turned out to be my last, as well as my first Worldwide Church of God service had it not been for a further mishap.

As we left the counseling room, Sian realized she had left her knitting in the car of the people who had brought us, who had been invited to visit another family from the congregation. Rather than take us along, they had arranged for others to take us home. We explained our dilemma to the sidekick, the gatekeeper of the counseling room. The man was a deacon in the congregation. Behind his gold-rimmed glasses, his kind eyes warmed to us; he knew where the people were, and would drive us over as soon as he was finished with his duties. When we arrived, the couple made their unexpected, uninvited guests feel welcome, and over the next few hours Sian and I experienced the opposite of what we had at services: warmth, camaraderie, laughter. We chatted with the adults, shared their pot-luck meal, and played with the small children. While the worship service had left an impression of what church should not be like, the rest of the afternoon stayed with me as a bright memory of what it could be like over the next twenty-two months until my second service.

At services, I had met a graduate student of comparative literature from Harvard, Arthur. For the rest of the summer I joined him, his roommate from Spain, and a grad student from England named Susan for meals (jacket and tie required for males, this was Harvard), so indirectly maintained contact with the church. When Susan learned where Arthur and I had met, she was curious to know more, but Arthur deflected as gracefully as he could.

My experience of services was shattering, but I did not

165

assume it was the fault of the church. Herbert Armstrong had published an autobiography and wrote in it of his first impressions of Church of God people in similar terms. He went on, though, to explain that he learned they were the salt of the earth; his reaction was due to his vanity, a desire to associate with only the finest people, in terms of wealth and success. Perhaps, I told myself, this was my problem as well. Wealth and success had less attraction for me though than they did for Armstrong; for me, the golden qualities were intelligence and culture. But my experience at the home of members suggested that perhaps Armstrong was right about the inner quality of the people.

Besides, just as fears of the H-bomb had weakened my resolve to stop reading *The Plain Truth* two years earlier, world events conspired to keep me convinced that the church was right in its predictions of an imminent end of the world. During my short visit home at the beginning of the summer, Margie woke me one morning to say that war had broken out in the Middle East. My immediate reaction was panic at the thought that I was not yet in the true church, for Worldwide's interpretation of the Book of Revelation convinced me that only its members, those who had responded to God's call, would be raised to meet Jesus when he returned to end the time of trouble that seemed surely to be beginning. Even though my first visit to services had not gone well, I continued writing out prescribed scriptures from the correspondence course and filled my Saturdays with reading the Bible and church literature.

It was also my first summer in a city. Living in a Gropius-designed dorm a few blocks from Harvard Square meant evenings filled with watching arthouse films at the Brattle, attending plays in a summer repertory, or listening to music at Club 47. The first time I saw Jim Kweskin's Jug Band perform, they served as backup band to Sippie Wallace, one of the many legends who recorded "race" records in the 1920s and then disappeared from view. Young blues aficionados rediscovered them and coaxed back on the stage as part of the continuing blues revival. When Pat Sky was there on another evening, I had my guitar with me —the evening had begun with an open mike. That night I gathered my courage and stayed after the show to jam with him and Jim Rooney. Sky became fascinated with my pawn-shop guitar and offered to trade it straight up for the Guild he was playing; he thought it would be just the guitar to retrofit with a resonator. I didn't take him up on it, feeling Sky might have regretted it when he woke the next morning if we had made the deal, but the offer deepened my sentimental attachment to it.

That summer I also put roll after roll of film into a 35 mm camera. It wasn't a very advanced model, had a fixed lens and neither rangefinder nor auto-focus. You had to estimate the distance to your object and turn a dial on the lens. My estimates weren't always accurate; especially in less-than-bright light, the results were soft and fuzzy. As with my interest in architecture, I had picked up the camera at Sian's urging. This suggestion fell on more fertile ground than the other. The most-discussed new film during my freshman year had been *Blow-Up*. We never got to the bottom of what the film meant—perhaps meaningless was the point, which resonated with my *Plain Truth*-filtered view of what was happening in the world—but it was clear that photographer was a cool thing to be, almost as cool as being an architect.

In those days using a small-format camera involved choosing between three kinds of film: color negative, color slides, or black-and-white. I tried all three, but with a prejudice against color, which seemed designed for what I dismissed as pretty pictures. Perhaps there was also a reaction to the slide shows we cousins had been subjected to by the older generation at family parties. Uncle George's slides of the trip to Europe in 1964, for example, were all properly exposed, in focus, and dull, seemingly taken only to demonstrate we had been there. I didn't know just what I wanted to do with a camera, but I was certain it would not be my uncle's photos. So my film of choice was black-and-white.

In addition to the aesthetic appeal, there was an economic factor. Color film had to be taken to a photo store, from which a week later the three-by-five-inch prints could be retrieved in a yellow envelope, with the negatives stored in a front pocket. Slides were sent away to Rochester, New York, in a yellow mailer. A few days later, the finished product arrived in your mailbox. Black-and-white film cost less to purchase and could be developed in a closet. My least developed skill is finger-dexterity; once on an aptitude test, I scored slightly above spastic. The fact that I could play guitar proved that anyone who tried hard enough could. Here was a new challenge. You set a light-tight black bag on a countertop, then placed in it a small metal canister, two double-spiral reels, a can opener, and the film you wanted to develop. You zipped the bag shut, stuck your hands through two circular openings trimmed in elastic, and set to work. I fumbled my way through many attempts, irreparably damaging a few rolls along the way, but finally learned to thread the roll of film onto the spiral reels. I didn't always manage to get the film exactly in the thread of the reel, many of those early negatives show chemical damage where two sections of the strip were threaded in the same groove. Once that was accomplished, and the lid safely placed on top of the canister, the bag could be unzipped. It was time to pour developing liquid through the light-tight lid, then after the prescribed time (which I usually counted out in my head—a darkroom timer would have been an additional expense), it was poured out and replaced by an acetic acid solution to stop the chemical developing process. That, in turn, was poured out and replaced by a third liquid designed to permanently affix the changes the chemicals had made to the film coating.

I photographed everything around me, from countless squirrels in Harvard Yard to Sian, who spent her meager pocket money on Vogue, posing in her wardrobe, usually in her Marimekko dresses from Design Research on Brattle Street. I pored through books by Henri Cartier-Bresson and others, a few instructional books, and some photography magazines, but otherwise, I was self-taught. I struggled with exposure, focus, and composition, then eagerly scanned the negative strips I developed, stoically swallowed my disappointment over the repeated difference between the photo I thought I had taken and the resulting image. Somehow over the course of the summer, my trial-and-error began to pay off, and there were a few shots I was happy with.

My writing had developed in the same trial-and-error way. From my first songs and poems in high school, a few remained that were less embarrassing than the others. Now I was growing increasingly confident and turned out more and more that I felt worth keeping.

The summer passed with no new word from Dylan, but the other group that had quietly broken up at the end

of the summer of 1966 beside mine, the Beatles, had re-
grouped, although purely as a studio band. Early in 1967
they released a single with two A-sides, immediately spark-
ing debates among fans: which was better, "Penny Lane"
or "Strawberry Fields Forever"? I thought both sides were
amazingly good but was firmly on the Strawberry Fields
side of the question. Both the song and the video they released in the absence of live performance had stretched
the notion of a "pop" song, and what it could do, while
somehow remaining popular. I didn't think the follow-up
LP, *Sgt. Pepper's Lonely Hearts Club Band*, was as strong, but
it grew on me over time. A few copies of the LP were available in England before the official U. S. release, so the first
I heard from it was "With a Little Help from My Friends,"
played on WBZ and breathlessly announced by the disc
jockey as being on a copy flown over the Atlantic. The LP
was defective, though, and the track skipped throughout
the length of the song. With the Beatles' love of experi-
mentation, however, I wasn't sure they hadn't taken scissors to the tape and intended the song to sound this way.

Another short visit home at the end of summer included a trip with Louise's family to their summer rental on a
lake in the Poconos. Louise was curious about my convictions, and early one morning we took our two Bibles and
rowed out to the middle of the lake and struggled our way
through Paul's letter to the Romans. Was the law in the

171

first five books of the Bible binding on Christians or wasn't it? She was open to hearing me out on why I thought it was, yet skeptical, and I was still a neophyte, so made a hash of my attempts to explain. Although not able to convince people close to me (Worldwide warned against trying), I remained confident I was on the right track and hoped one day to be a part of the church, even though it and I had not hit it off at first.

Chapter Seven

I thought no more of transferring to Ambassador College after one year in Boston; neither my parents nor I brought it up. Nor did I follow through on the possibility of a transfer to Harvard for my last two years as I returned to Boston University in the fall of 1967 for my sophomore year; fear of rejection held me back.

As every year, the crisp fall weather brought fresh resolve to keep up with assigned reading, faithfully attend lectures and not wait to start papers until the night before a deadline. This year holding to it was easier, at least for two of my classes. After my disappointment with lectures the first year, I listened for a semester to one of B. U.'s stars, Murray Levin, in an introductory course in U. S. politics. Andy and I took the class together, scavenged for seats in over-filled Hayden Auditorium, and reveled in Levin's performances as he stalked the stage, delivering his tightly-structured lectures without notes. We waited in vain for him to lose his way after announcing his first point with a clear, high-pitched "one." After forty-five minutes of argument, example, anecdote and aside, by which time we were sure he didn't know what followed, his voice rang out "two." He was not only a brilliant lecturer; he was a perceptive scholar. As he analyzed the results of the most recent local Boston elections, he concluded that the New Deal coalition was crumbling, a thesis borne out a year later in the presidential election when Alabama governor George Wallace mounted a third-party challenge that split the Democratic Party, carrying not only southern states but finishing disturbingly well in northern cities.

I assiduously took notes. Unlike others, who outfitted themselves with spiral-bound notebooks for each course, my selective frugality led me to favor the cheapest of loose newsprint sheets, which I folded lengthwise to fill each side with long, narrow columns embellished with caricatures of the lecturer, fellow students, or fantasy figures. After class, I unfolded the sheets and placed them in manila folders, one for each class.

As good as Levin was, he was matched in my estimation by another. Sian and I settled in with anticipation for each animated lecture from Robert Sproat on modern English literature. The ambitious reading list provided my first exposure to authors such as D. H. Lawrence and James Joyce, as well as deepened acquaintance with authors I had already read such as Joseph Conrad and William Faulkner. A delightful discovery was Gerard Manley Hopkins, drunk on God and words, and, as spring rolled around, Ezra Pound and the other Imagists. Here, too, I was frugal. Sian and I bought one paperback copy of the books on the course reading list and took turns reading them. While my papers were still poorly-structured and the observations superficial, the reading, discussions with Sian, and Sproat's lectures were a highlight of my Boston years.

Along with another SPC core course, Fundamentals of Communication Research, my introduction to statistical analysis, content analysis, and other arcane matters, and the second semester of calculus, I took the first of two semesters of physics. Mechanics bored me, but my first exposure to relativity and quantum mechanics held endless fascination, although this failed to translate into a good grade. Instead, it provided hours of contemplation, as I tried to integrate these insights into my understanding of God. Herbert Armstrong, Albert Einstein, Gerard Manley Hopkins: a strange mixture. The common denominator was that it wasn't the picture of God I had as a child.

Fall also brought another side interest. At Sian's encouragement, I enrolled for cello lessons at a private music school in Cambridge. Her circle of friends included a couple of cellists, Tina, who had the vivacious beauty of Jacqueline du Pré, and Ronnie, who joined the ranks of the

Boston Symphony Orchestra as an undergraduate. So this became another element in her image of her dream man: a cello-playing architect and photographer. It wouldn't have been bad, to round out the picture, if I smoked a pipe as well. I enjoyed the lessons and practiced diligently, but nineteen is a bit old to take up a string instrument, so I stopped after a year. Of all her hopes for me, only that of becoming a photographer stuck.

I signed up to return to the same dorm room, but none of my roommates had, and the new ones were difficult to warm to. Meanwhile, friends from SPC had arranged to live in the room next door; Andy, Len, and a third, Charley. It soon seemed to them that they had made a mistake with the fourth roommate and after a few weeks asked if I would like to switch with him. I agreed immediately; dorm life became more congenial.

Much of my social life revolved around Sian's friends; one set was those with whom she had gone to a convent school. One was just back from an obscure college in Kansas, where she had become pregnant, returning to the Boston area to deliver the child at a home for unwed mothers; it was put up for adoption. Another had gone to France to study at the Sorbonne. Home on a visit, she seemed the embodiment of sophistication as she sat on the edge of my bed, smoking Gauloises and telling of the Paris of Sartre and Simone de Beauvoir. I took a particular liking

176

to a third, Karen, warm-hearted, tall, slim but strongly-built. She worked in a shop off Harvard Square; Sian and I dropped in from time to time, we also visited her in the apartment she shared with Oscar in a brick row house in the South End.

Sian's other circle was her SFA colleagues, especially Cathy and her boyfriend, Alan. A tall, lanky boy with an untamed shock of straight blond hair, from a Quaker family, he was a composition student; I heard that Gardner Read, the theory and composition professor, felt he was the best student he had taught. I spent evenings at Alan's apartment listening to recordings of some of Alan's favorite twentieth-century music. The shock of my first exposure to Bartók had worn off, and I listened to what I heard with an open mind, and often enjoyment. This reaction intrigued Alan; many of his fellow students played this music as part of their coursework but didn't like it. Sian's circle of SFA friends included a few non-musicians as well; there was Margo, a graphic artist and sculptress, and Jackie, a drama student.

Between the two semesters, Sian went with me for the Christmas break, as she had for Thanksgiving that year. We saw little of each other in the daytime, though. While she knit, read, and practiced the piano, I worked long hours at the store, as Thanksgiving, Christmas and New Year provided good business. I stood for ten to twelve hours next to

Fooled into Thinking

Charlie at a back sandwich counter preparing party trays. Despite the hard work, which also left little time for socializing with friends while back in my hometown, I enjoyed these hours. Charlie had worked hard to build up the store, which allowed for little time at home, and little energy for interacting with his children. By working alongside him, I finally was able to get to know him better.

In the days between Christmas and New Year, at the end of 1967, Dylan released an album, his first since *Blonde on Blonde*, eighteen months earlier. The timing of the release seemed as if he wanted it to escape notice. Record companies typically timed releases by their major artists for the month before Christmas, which made it easy for parents to decide what to give their adolescent children. Dylan insisted that CBS dispense with the usual marketing and advertising. Even more surprising was the content of *John Wesley Harding*. A year-and-a-half after delivering a masterpiece of dense-sounding rock music, on this album he relied on a simply strummed acoustic guitar, harmonica, and subdued drum and bass. On the last two tracks, there was also a steel guitar. The disc not only stood in contrast to his last one, but this was a half-year after the Beatles had set a new benchmark for complexity with *Sgt. Pepper*. It seemed perverse. As my friends and I repeatedly listened, though, the songs revealed their depth. The title track was Dylan's contribution to the sub-genre of outlaw songs; the Carter Family had sung of John Hardy, Woody Guthrie wrote of fellow Oklahoman Pretty Boy Floyd, but the tradition stretched back to Robin Hood. The most-discussed film in those months was Arthur Penn's *Bonnie and Clyde*. Dylan's protagonist, too, "was never known to hurt an honest man." It was criminality as an exercise in social justice. Gone was the druggy, surrealistic imagery that had saturated his songs for the previous three years. Trapped next to the thief where there seemed to be no way out, nailed to a cross, for instance, was the Joker ("All Along the Watchtower"). The Joker is the card that doesn't belong in the deck. When it's nevertheless thrown in, it changes the rules of the game. Ironically, it's the thief, though, who remonstrates to the Joker that, unlike what many feel, life is not a joke. Since "the hour is getting late," it is time for straight talk, honest words, the plain truth. Sometimes the best place to hide is in plain sight. Together with the religious undertones of some of the other songs—Augustine recast as a martyr, Tom Paine as a secular saint, even the banter between the two main characters in the shaggy dog "Frankie Lee and Judas Priest"—there was an earnest moral subtext to these sparse songs, a parallel morality—with a counterpart in his idiosyncratic grammar—to that of a mainstream society that was raining napalm down on a distant land.

The campus was not immune to the growing nation-

wide protests over the Vietnam War. When students returned to classes after the Christmas break for spring
semester, the turbulence seemed to accelerate. In neighboring New Hampshire, Senator Eugene McCarthy did the
unthinkable, challenging an incumbent president of his
party, one who had won a record-setting landslide victory
just four years earlier, and nearly defeated him in the primary in February. After this, Robert F. Kennedy, who had
been even more vocal in his opposition to the war, but had
shied away from confrontation, joined the race. I watched
the live coverage of his announcement in my dorm's television room, convinced he would be the last U. S. president
before the great tribulation. At the end of March, after a
surprisingly heavy and well-coordinated Viet Cong offen-
sive upset predictions of their imminent defeat, Lyndon
Johnson announced he would not seek reelection.

We had hardly digested this news when Martin Luther
King, Jr. was assassinated in Memphis. While we shared the
outrage of most Americans, the campus community was
particularly affected since King had received his doctor-
ate from B. U. just fifteen years before and many cherished
personal memories of his time there. It was as if time stood
still for the next few days, as violence spread through the
country, and I became more convinced that this world
could not last much longer. The writers in *The Plain Truth*,
like those of *The Watchtower*, who were also peddling the

same date, 1975, for the end of the world, were sure that it was so. It turned out that Dylan was closer to the mark; there were only two riders approaching to the sound of howling wind, not all four horsemen. The hour was indeed late, but it was not the last hour. I didn't know it at the time and continued my diligent study in the hopes of someday being part of the true church.

Spring returned to Boston. As the year before, as the piles of cinder-inflected crystalline snow shrank and the evenings lengthened, it became possible, for a few hours at a time, to forget the imminent end of the world. Leaves budded, then flourished on the trees, and I explored my creativity. Alan asked me to write the libretto for an opera, an intimidating project. Typically, I started by working my way through a book on the history of opera, then never got around to finishing the libretto. Andy came across a satirical book telling the story of Lyndon Johnson in a parody of Biblical prose, *The Begatting of the President*. He contacted the author, got an option to record it, and went into the studio with a DJ for M. I. T.'s college radio station we admired. Nothing came of the finished product. Even the record that came out after Andy's option expired quickly sank into obscurity, despite featuring the formidable voice of Orson Welles.

As the weather improved, Andy and I were often out with our cameras, I with my 35 mm, he with his Rolleiflex.

Fooled into Thinking

We rigged a makeshift darkroom that we could set up and take down in our bathroom and spent hours making our prints. We also developed another partnership. Andy had been in a band in high school in his hometown on Long Island and had spent a summer working in one of the offices in the Brill Building, the legendary song factory at Broadway and 49th Street in Manhattan. He planned to major in film but spent spare time working out melodies and song structures on the piano. He liked my lyrics, and we began collaborating.

In addition to songwriting and photo excursions, we talked for hours on end. Like me, Andy learned through dialogue. He was fascinated by my beliefs; his encounters with Christians and Christianity up to then had not impressed him. He found it interesting that the Worldwide Church of God was open to the Jewish roots of Christianity. Christians often seemed oblivious to the fact that Jesus was born and died a Jew, which may have been a factor in the lack of outcry to the Holocaust just three decades earlier. The Worldwide Church of God, on the other hand, saw this as a key to understanding his message. Also, the church had a teaching about the purpose of life. Given that Herbert Armstrong always wrote as if his insights were directly given by God through his reading solely of the Bible, it was years before I learned of the similarities of this teaching to the tradition in Greek theology of *theopoiesis*, which

182

explains the purpose of incarnation as God becoming man so that man could become God. The idea of human life as a training ground to become god-like appealed to Andy and corresponded to what he had heard in lectures in the psychology course he was taking from Willem Pinard. It was only after becoming a member of the church that I came to understand that in Armstrong's literal-minded teaching, the idea had grown to mean that humans were destined to become gods. The theological and philosophical problems with this only became clear to me over time.

The school year drew to a close, and Sian and I planned again to spend the summer together, this time in Westfield. I arranged for her to stay in Keith's home, as he would be away for the summer, and she found a job in a newly-opened clothing boutique, while I went back to work in my dad's delicatessen. Our relationship continued the emotional ups and downs it had since the beginning. Our shared interest in Christianity was riven by a difference of opinion. She clung to the hope that I might yet convert to Catholicism. She encouraged me to supplement my diet of Worldwide Church of God publications with works by others; ideally Catholics such as Augustine and Newman (both converts), but failing that, serious Protestants. At her urging, I read Karl Barth's *The Word of God and the Word of Man*. We followed the second Vatican council and its aftermath closely. One development allowed interfaith couples to marry without the non-Catholic promising that children would be raised Catholic. Another reinterpreted the requirement of Sunday church attendance to allow Saturday evening services to count. She was especially encouraged by this; for much of the year, I could attend a worship service on the Sabbath by going to mass. We bought, read and discussed a book by Charles Davis, an English Catholic theologian who left the church in frustration that the renewal of Vatican II had not gone far enough in restoring the ethos of love that characterized the early Christian community, as well as the rebuttal by Gregory Baum (he subsequently left the church as well).

Aside from the stress in our relationship over religion, and the emotional upheavals due to our relative immaturity, there was tension arising from our unfulfilled sex drive as well. We both believed that premarital intercourse would be wrong. In my case, this stemmed from the teachings of the Worldwide Church of God, in hers, feelings of right and wrong reinforced by the fears of pregnancy instilled by twelve years of being taught by nuns. Besides, despite her critical attitude toward aspects of her church, it remained important to her to take the Eucharist, but before doing so, she would have to recount whatever we had done in a confessional. We shared ample affection, but drew the line, sometimes with difficulty, at "going all the way," in the phrase of the time. Most often this was by mu-

184

tual consent, but at times in spite of the insistent urge of one or the other.

That fall we returned to Boston a few days before classes were to resume. Andy, Charlie and I had decided to leave the dorm and had rented an apartment a few blocks away from campus. That summer I had designed plywood furniture to fit the dimensions of my room. My dad and I drove it up and assembled it. There was a tall bookcase that fit between a window and the door to the back porch overlooking a train line, and a row of lower shelves to fit under a bank of windows overlooking an alley along a second wall. It doubled as the bench for sitting at the square table I used for my desk. I even constructed a bed. It was my dad's idea to place a plywood X under the middle of it, cut a little lower than the level of the bed to make use of the natural flexibility of plywood, eliminating the need for a box spring. All it needed was a mattress. A headboard behind the bed had a shelf that held an alarm clock, a radio, and a reading lamp.

Andy's mother was an interior designer; together they had planned the color scheme of the entire apartment. As soon as I arrived, we three roommates set to work painting. The bathroom presented a unique challenge. The ceiling showed water damage that had never been repaired. Andy's mother suggested we paint it black, reasoning that eyes are never drawn to what is dark if there is something

185

bright to focus on, for instance, the yellow we painted the bathroom walls. The apartment featured a pantry next to the kitchen, and Andy and I turned that into a darkroom by hanging Naugahyde curtains with velcro strips that when closed made the two passageways light-tight. It took a lot of work to finish before classes started. We worked late, night after night, and late Friday night (that is, on the Sabbath), Andy and Charley found me stretched out in the bathtub in a half-sleep, with my hand waving a paintbrush filled with yellow paint in the air.

As we worked, we played our newest records. The melancholy mood of Joni Mitchell's debut album fit the waning days of summer, turning to another New England fall. Even the rare upbeat song, "Night in the City," expressed a yearning, an urge not to miss out on life. Sometimes the sadness she sought to evoke was best captured in a concrete observation, as when Marcy "stops a postman passing by." The roomy sound of the production made her unusually-tuned guitar seem larger. Other favorites were Judy Collins' *Wildflowers*, Tom Rush's *The Circle Game*, and Eric Andersen's *More Hits from Tin Can Alley*, all of which supplemented acoustic guitars with classical instruments. I particularly liked the arrangements on *Wildflowers* by Joshua Rifkin, part of the newly-burgeoning movement that championed Baroque music.

Junior year meant that it was time to declare majors.

Andy chose film, Charley, broadcasting; I opted for journalism. I had spent some of my summer earnings to up-
grade to a Nikkormat, Nikon's entry-level camera, and put
many rolls of film through it. The school offered a concentration in photojournalism within the journalism degree program, I submitted a portfolio and was accepted.
This meant working closely with a small group of other
photographers, many of whom went on to make names
for themselves in the field. It also meant four semesters of
classes with Harris Smith, a soft-spoken, perceptive professor. He was from the mid-west, but fit perfectly in New
England. An early riser, he spent hours wandering among
the dunes and ponds of Ipswich, where he had made his
home. I thought of him as Thoreau with a camera.

He set assignments that seemed at the time uncre-
ative, but I was amazed in later years how often I was confronted with a problem in taking the photo I needed, a
challenge that one of his exercises had been designed to
help deal with.

As school started, the presidential campaign went
into full swing. Richard Nixon, who had narrowly lost to
JFK eight years earlier, and then after failing to be elected
governor of California in 1962 promised the press they
wouldn't have him to kick around anymore, had become
the Republican candidate. George Wallace's candidacy
drew a disturbing amount of support outside of the South,

including in Boston. That fall the nominee of the Democratic Party, Vice-President Hubert H. Humphrey, made a campaign appearance in the heart of the downtown shopping district. I went with my camera and took photos, primarily of the students demonstrating against the Viet Nam War. On a whim, I went the following Monday evening to the darkroom of the campus newspaper and turned my film over to Peter Simon, the photo editor. The *B. U. News* had assigned one of its staff photographers to cover the rally, so none of my photos ran that week, but Peter looked carefully at the strip of negatives after it came out of the developing chemicals, and put my name down for an assignment for the next week's issue.

From then on, I shot photos for three different purposes: my class projects, my *News* assignments, and my personal work. The *News* had been controversial ever since I arrived on campus, and served to prepare many for careers, not only in journalism, both counter-cultural and mainstream but also in television and the emerging field of rock journalism. Now I too was one of the denim-clad, shaggy-haired Newsniks. I shared their reflexive suspicion of what any establishment institution propounded since it intersected in some way with the insistent headlines of articles in *The Plain Truth*.

On Monday nights, the *News* darkroom became my second home. Peter's grainy images, produced by pushing

188

Kodak's fastest black-and-white film, Tri-X, to a sensitivity more than twice of its rating, printed on high contrast Ilford paper, became my new aesthetic standard. I studied him as he worked, and over time, Peter entrusted developing some of his prints to me, which I felt was a great honor. I learned much about photography watching these images emerge under my hands in a tray of chemicals. Peter had a gift for the eloquent image—the flower planted in the mud or the war veteran in World War I uniform and helmet standing in the middle of student anti-war protesters. Other staff photographers, none of them SPC photojournalism majors, supplemented my education. Through the long nights, as we worked, Peter's tape recorder provided a carefully selected soundtrack, my first exposure to groups such as the Incredible String Band. For Peter, it was a plus that I clearly remembered an LP that his sisters Lucy and Carly had put out in the mid-sixties that had received some airplay on a folk music program on WCBS before sinking to obscurity. This was before Carly's breakthrough in the early seventies.

It was from that tape recorder that I learned Dylan hadn't been inactive in the interim between *Blonde on Blonde* and *John Wesley Harding*. Peter had a copy of the first successful bootleg, the *Great White Wonder*. One highlight was a set of performances from 1961, made during a trip home to Minnesota for a short visit, shortly before he went into the Columbia studios for the first time, show-ing an inventive stamp on an assortment of folk and blues songs. An out-take from his *Freewheelin'* sessions, a wild rock & roll song, "Mixed-Up Confusion," showed that "go-ing electric" had been an option for him all along. More fascinating yet were the tracks that have become known as *The Basement Tapes*. These murkily-recorded songs, done together with the Hawks in a tract house near Woodstock, shared the same back-to-the-roots ethos of the collection of songs on *Harding* but were wider in conception, by turns raucous, ribald, sly, and profoundly moral. Some songs had been released on the debut LP of the former Hawks, now simply the Band, *Music from Big Pink*, others on *Sweetheart of the Rodeo*, the record on which Gram Parsons joined the Byrds, which had reinvented itself a country-rock band. Still others would soon appear in covers by Manfred Mann and Peter, Paul and Mary. Dylan's fountain of inspiration had clearly not run dry.

It was during one of the darkroom sessions that I re-lented and took a turn as a joint was passed around. It was my second acquaintance, the first having been while visit-ing Karen's partner during his after-midnight jazz show on the University's FM-radio station. On that first oc-casion, just before flying home for a school break, I had thought it hadn't affected me at all. Only when I developed the photos I had taken the next morning before leaving for the airport could I see that it had done something to my perception. Still, I hadn't repeated the experience until this late-night, late-winter darkroom session. I not only took my turn, I greedily awaited the next toke. Meanwhile, I was wearing the headphones plugged into Peter's tape recorder, a new experience that delivered the music more directly into my head than ambient sound in the room did. I was sharply focused as Dylan sang "It's All Over Now, Baby Blue," and noticed a malevolence in his voice I had never heard before. Or when I had heard it, it was in bitter put-downs such as "Like a Rolling Stone" and "Positively Fourth Street." Now I heard it while Dylan delivered a line in which I previously had heard tenderness. The combination of the two experiences—my hunger for the next toke and the feeling I heard in Dylan's voice—made me decide there would be no third time. My experience with alcohol had shown me it was something I could enjoy or leave alone, now I sensed something different, something that could be stronger than I.

Despite all that was going on in my life, I did attend classes. My favorite that semester was a course in poetry writing taught by John Malcolm Brinnin, legendary as companion and chronicler of Dylan Thomas's last days, but also a noted poet in his own right. In previous semesters, I had taken part in extracurricular poetry workshops, one led by Jan Dyroff, a young graduate assistant, the other by Elizabeth ("Ma") Barker, a professor in the English department. But this was in another league. To be admitted to the class, you had to submit a portfolio and be interviewed. There was some competition for places; I was the only non-English major that semester. It intrigued Brinnin that I majored in photography; he suggested I should assemble a book of poems and photos in which the two complemented rather than illustrated each other on facing pages, a project that got no further than the libretto for Alan. Getting admitted to the course was only part of the challenge. Students were assigned to write a poem a week, each using an increasingly complex form, such as villanelle and pantoum, with the result to read like a poem, not merely an exercise. I scribbled lines and ideas in a notebook I always carried with me, pored over the many volumes of the *Oxford English Dictionary* to find fresh words, and experienced the satisfaction of working diligently on the challenge. In academics, I continued to be more of a sprinter than a long-distance runner. This was one of the few courses that held my interest throughout a semester.

Among my other courses was Newswriting and Reporting, taught by Norm Moyes, an experienced newspaperman. My motivation and interest varied, and one day I skipped class to spend the fine fall afternoon walking around town. The group was small enough that I would be missed, so I felt the need to fabricate an excuse. I stopped at the Mugar Library and stumbled into the opening of an exhibit of Piet Hein's Grooks. Hein was a Danish designer who had begun creating these combinations of drawings and aphoristic poems while active in the Resistance during the Second World War. Among his design achievements was the super-ellipse, a formula that made maximum use of a space without using square corners. I blended into the group touring the exhibit, had the chance to talk with him, took a few photos, and wrote it up. Moyes was pleased with the result and suggested I submit it to the *Boston Globe Sunday Magazine*, and the article was accepted. The day after it ran, Moyes proudly took me to meet the department head. I spent the $75 payment at a store on Harvard Square for an antique ring for Sian, a Victorian design of a large, raised, oval pink tourmaline set in gold and surrounded by smaller pale green tourmaline stones, our engagement ring, although we still did not make an official announcement.

Yet our relationship was changing. She had moved with her family from Brookline to a less-expensive apartment in Arlington, which meant spending less time at her place. I was no longer in a dorm, where visiting hours for members of the opposite sex were strictly limited, so we could spend time at my apartment. But overall, we were together less than before. Aside from my Monday nights in the darkroom, we both noticed the increased workload, now that we were juniors. And perhaps the emotional roller coaster was wearing on both.

We spent the Christmas break together in Westfield, then returned to Boston for spring semester. For me, this meant a second semester in newswriting, with a different teacher, one I had a harder time appreciating than Moyes. His professional experience had been with a tabloid; one day he came into class enthused over the murder of a coed, and the suggestion of voodoo ritual police had discovered in her apartment. "What a story!" he exclaimed. It was one of the moments when I sensed I didn't have what it would take to be a successful newspaperman and hoped I never would.

Another course, Design in Communication, was one of the few that motivated me throughout an entire semester. While more directly relevant to those who hoped to go on to a career in advertising after graduation, the teacher was a sharp-eyed, encouraging pro who could communicate her love of applying simple design principles to great effect. Together with a course in Aesthetics that I also took that semester, my eye was becoming schooled, not that the results always paid off immediately as I continued to struggle with the challenge of Harris Smith's demanding weekly photography assignments. He chided when he saw that a student had not left a print long enough in the fixer solution, encouraging us that if we were careful in our craftsmanship, we might create an artifact that long outlived us. His was the ethos that built cathedrals. He set high standards, and my results—faults in exposure, focus, composition, or sloppy darkroom technique—were on display with brutal objectivity when we showed our prints in class. I was learning, but not as quickly as the others, and my grades reflected it.

Best of all that semester was a course reading Tolstoy in translation. I had never until that time been so completely drawn into a world created by mere words as when I read *War and Peace* for the first time. The epic sweep and sharply-drawn individuals cast a spell on me, and his other works, not only *Anna Karenina* but also many of the novellas, had an almost equal effect.

A small unexpected package from California arrived in the mail one day from Mike, my high school bandmate. He had sent a copy of the first single released by the new group he was part of, called the Millennium, of all things—the time of peace and joy I was anticipating.

I continued to make time soon after waking each morning for Bible reading, supplemented by the correspondence course and booklets from Ambassador College. One of the booklets contrasted the traditional Christian holidays such as Christmas and Easter, which, it asserted, were pagan in origin and displeasing to God, with the holy days whose observance was commanded to ancient Israel.

Andy was able to fill in a bit of the background of how they were celebrated from his upbringing. In the fall, I observed these holy days on my own, fasting on the Day of Atonement, praying that by the following year, I would be with the church as it kept the eight-day Feast of Tabernacles.

In addition to the stress this caused in my relationship with Sian, there was an internal pressure as well. By this time the church had found a Boston outlet for its daily radio program. I arranged my lunch break so that I was in our apartment to listen. What I heard, though, was often hard to swallow. Garner Ted Armstrong was a gifted speaker, with a convincing tone of voice and a colorful vocabulary. His programs were not scripted; his father wrote in *The Plain Truth* with fatherly pride how his son would dash into the studio, often with no more than an idea of how he would open. Often he would go for days following a tangent. More than once in those months he spoke of the turmoil on campuses across the country and contrasted it with the peaceful haven that was Ambassador College. I, however, was torn and distressed. While I yearned to experience the ideal Armstrong portrayed, it was also clear that much of what he said was ill-informed and bigoted. So deeply was I hooked at that time, though, that I dropped to my knees and prayed for the strength not to turn the radio off and reject God's messenger.

In the end, it wasn't about the thousands of others on

my campus, nor the many more on other campuses. It was about me, and my struggles to live a life in which I aligned not only my actions but even my thoughts with God's law, the Ten Commandments. I didn't place much stock in dreams, but one night had an unusually vivid one that left me disturbed long after I awoke. In this dream, I was the one who killed John F. Kennedy. As the dream drew to a close, I was appalled to find the rifle in my hands, shocked at what I had done. Awake, I realized that even if I hadn't been the one to pull the trigger, given the right circumstances, I was capable of that or any other enormity. I knelt at my bedside and tearfully prayed that if living meant continuing to try to live as God wanted and failing, then I would rather not live.

I waited impatiently for the Passover and the first Day of Unleavened Bread to end, telephoned Reg Platt and said I was ready to resume visiting services. He asked about Sian; I said we were still together, but that becoming part of the church was more important to me than my relationship with her. He said he would seek advice from Raymond Cole, and called back the next day with Cole's Solomonic decree. I did not have to break up with Sian to return to services, but only inform her of my decision, and let her decide what she wanted to do about it. If she, like Ruth following Naomi, decided to consent to stay with me on that basis, then it would be no hindrance to membership.

197

On an early morning in April, two-and-a-half years after we met and fell in love, I told her my intention. She wished me well, said goodbye, turned around and walked away. I didn't dwell on what her abrupt response might mean. I knew her well enough to sense that in her mind, she was practicing renunciation, giving me up for God. But if she were inwardly relieved to be rid of me, I didn't want to know it. If on the other hand, her pain was as deep or even deeper than mine, that would have been worse. There is a clue in the portraits taken later that week for next year's yearbook. Our two faces show pain, mingled with a yearning to do whatever God willed.

We never saw each other after that day. There were books, records, and a turntable to pick up from her family's apartment; I went a few months later, when she was out, her father and I making awkward small-talk. As it turned out, some of my books and records remained in Arlington, and some of the books she set aside for me were those I had bought for her. There is no way to clearly untangle the artifacts of a relationship, even one that lasted as briefly as ours, and in which we never set up a common household. I only heard from her once after that, a pleasant letter asking how I was doing. I was afraid of being drawn back to seeing her, so asked Platt for advice. He said that there would be nothing wrong in replying in the same manner she had written, but I had trouble finding the right words, put it off, and eventually lost the letter before answering.

I attended services the following Saturday, this time part of a carpool of people who lived in the city. The driver was Frank, who lived in a small apartment in Brookline, and whose marriage had broken up when he came into the church. There was a woman, the widow of a Baptist minister, recently retired from being an executive secretary at one of the banks on State Street, and a woman from Roxbury with her young daughter. By now, the congregation had grown and was meeting in two locations, Concord, New Hampshire, and Sudbury, a suburb of Boston. This group met in a school auditorium, a distinct improvement from the Odd Fellows Hall in Manchester. This time there was no traumatic reaction to the experience. The following week at the close of services, Platt announced that there would be a meeting for those ready to be baptized at the side of the auditorium. I didn't know that when he said "ready," he meant in the minister's assessment, after some counseling sessions; I understood it from my perspective. After my years of struggle, and now at the cost of my relationship, I was ready to commit.

Platt did a small but noticeable double-take when he saw me in the group, but let me stay. We were told where we were to meet the next day, and that we were to bring a towel and a change of clothes. Rides were organized, since we were to travel to a farm in Western Massachusetts.

There, standing in a horse trough, I declared that I had repented of my sins and accepted Jesus Christ as my savior, and was immersed in cold April ground water.

I had been baptized—sprinkled—as an infant in a Lutheran service with Uncle George and Charlie's older sister, Tante Tiene, as god-parents. In keeping with its literalistic reading of scripture, the Worldwide Church of God denied that this was a baptism. In the New Testament, baptism was a choice, a decision that followed repentance, and was for the remission of sins. Finding no Biblical warrant for the teaching of original sin, it taught that in the case of an infant there were no sins to remit. Worldwide never noticed that their view of the human nature in every newborn child was even darker than that of Augustine when he formulated the original sin teaching. In their understanding, human nature was not a stain to be washed away, but an evil drive to be countered by parental discipline, then repented of and struggled against over a lifetime. Even in the case of those who had been baptized in a manner they felt followed Biblical precedent, that is, after a conversion experience as older adolescents or as adults, the church almost never recognized it as valid, since in most cases the sins repented of did not include failure to keep the Sabbath. Moreover, a valid baptism was followed in their view by a second act, in which a minister laid hands on the head of the newly baptized to pray that they would receive the

Holy Spirit, necessary for becoming a child of God and resisting human nature. How could someone who was not a minister of the true church convey this gift? So although Worldwide did not, strictly speaking, teach that only its baptism was valid, in practice it was the rule.

It would be years before I learned that Herbert Armstrong had been an exception to his own rule. Through his contact with the Church of God in Oregon in the 1920s, he had become convinced of his need to be re-baptized but was loath to admit the spiritual authority of the elders in the local congregation. Rather than accept baptism from them, he convinced a local Baptist minister to perform the act, but avowedly not for the purpose of taking up membership in that minister's congregation. It was an act that said much about him. He resisted the need to accept any other man's authority, yet relished exercising his own. Dictating the terms on which he would be baptized could well raise a question as to whether he had the humble, teachable mind that he decreed was a necessary prerequisite.

I have never questioned that what I went through in those early spring days of 1969 was a genuine conversion experience. Sadly, the Worldwide Church of God was not geared to help me understand this as an actualization of promises that had been made, and a commitment that had been undertaken on my behalf, on the day of my first baptism almost twenty-one years earlier.

The decision to risk my relationship with Sian was made easier by a growing friendship with another girl, Susan. A good friend of Andy's girl, Carla, she was a soft-spoken, soft-eyed girl with a protruding lower lip that gave the impression she was brooding over some secret all her own. An English major and aspiring writer, she was from a non-conventional, but spiritual household and her curiosity had been aroused in the previous months, before meeting me, as Andy described my critical posture toward "Churchianity." We met, traded songs and poems, and a friendship grew. One night, in the week between my first and second service, after a tumultuous argument with one of her roommates, she rang my bell, and like Boaz to Ruth, I covered her to shelter her in my bed. Andy underscored the night with Dylan's newly released *Nashville Skyline* and its centerpiece song, "Lay, Lady, Lay."

Classes had ended the Friday before my baptism. The new so-called "reading period" between the end of classes and the beginning of exams was a flurry of activity, turning in assignments and having conferences with professors. My parents had given me a car on my previous visit home, an early twenty-first birthday present, and I decided to fit in a quick trip home on Wednesday for their anniversary. It would give me a chance to tell them in person of my break-up and baptism. That morning my photo class met to receive feedback on our semester project portfolios, but finally, I was able to leave shortly after noon. This put me in heavy traffic as I reached the Garden State Parkway in New Jersey. A light rain began to fall, but traffic was moving well. Suddenly my car started to swerve as I rounded a curve on a hill. I tried to correct, but the car overreacted to whatever I tried to do. I finally took my hands off the wheel, cried out an urgent, brief prayer, and the car steadied. I had been in the middle lane. The car veered into the left lane, then back to the middle, then to the right, finally hitting a clump of bushes on the side of the road, spinning around, striking the bushes again and coming to a stop on the side of the road, with me looking at the oncoming traffic, stunned and wondering how I had managed to not hit any other of the many cars on the road.

A tow truck came and hooked up the car. I climbed into the cab for the remainder of the trip. The Rambler dealer who had sold it to Charlie examined it and exonerated me—a defective ball bearing in the steering column was to blame. That explained the cause, but it didn't explain how I had escaped unscathed without involving anyone else in the accident. Coming within days of my baptism, which according to Paul's letter to the Romans symbolizes the death of the old man and the beginning of a new life, this seemed more than coincidental, and the inexplicable steadying of the car and safe deposit in a clump of bushes—had I come to the side shortly before or shortly after,

203

I would have hit a railing, with no cushioning—seemed nothing less than divine intervention. My life from that day was a gift, a gift I owed to God. The dealer gave a good price on a better-quality replacement, and on Friday I headed back to Boston to take my exams. As soon as they were finished, I headed back to New Jersey for another short visit.

Andy and I had continued collaborating on songs, sometimes working on an old dust-covered piano we found in the basement of our apartment building, sometimes in our rooms, with him creating melodies on his recorder. We had a sheaf of songs we were pleased with, and our friends were encouraging. Susan told her brother, an upcoming producer for Columbia Records, and he arranged for us to audition at one of Columbia's publishing houses. We spent a day in New York making the rounds, starting at the Brill Building, where Andy had interned. To stand in the lobby and read the nameplates on the directory—for example, "Domino, Fats"—was to breathe in the history of pop music. We went up to see Phil Margo (Andy had worked for him). He liked our songs, suggested a chord change to one, and wished us well. We continued to RCA, where the reception was much cooler, but the man who listened offered to purchase one particular song. His choice didn't impress us; it was a parody of a couple of Marvin Gaye hits that we had done quickly and wasn't representative of our style.

The highlight of the day was the visit Susan's brother had arranged at April-Blackwood. We had an appointment with Tony Orlando, who was working there as an A&R man between his solo career and his career revival. The only false note of our visit was when I recalled the show he had headlined with our band on the bill. "Don't remind me," he cried out, "those were the worst years of my life!" At that time, the hits had stopped coming, and he was headlining shows in places such as our local school. He quickly recovered his natural friendliness, though, and showed us around. He introduced us to a man working in a nearby office barely big enough for an upright piano and a stool. He was a show business lifer, having started with writing arrangements for big bands in the 1940s. I knew his name from reading the labels of hits he had co-written for Cameo-Parkway artists in the early sixties. As we auditioned, we could hear him in the next room, working on a lead-sheet for James Taylor's "Rainy Day Man." April-Blackwood had the publishing rights to Taylor's songs. I felt we were in the heart of the music business.

We went through our entire sheaf of songs, and Orlando grew more excited with each. "You guys are the next Simon and Garfunkel," he enthused. It was my first exposure to the phrase, common currency not only in the music business but in Hollywood as well. Few are looking for the first; most are looking for the next. His closing words as we prepared to leave his office, "I really want to work with you guys," were a welcome culmination to our day in New York.

That it didn't come to anything had to do with the different turns each of our lives took. Orlando soon had a song land on his desk he felt was so good that he into the studio and to record himself with two backup singers. At the time, he was not sure he wanted to resume his career, so he released it anonymously, under the name Dawn. The record, coincidentally produced by Phil Margo, became a big hit. Andy, frustrated with the documentary-oriented approach of the film department of B.U., had been accepted for a summer course at U.S.C., which would put him in touch with Hollywood professionals. He came back with a stylish new haircut, a beard, and an option on a book he wanted to film, *The Harrad Experiment*. I was caught up in being part of the Worldwide Church of God.

A repeated theme in sermons I heard there was a warning about entanglement with "the world." Susan tried to understand, though disturbed by my rabid outburst about illegitimate babies mortared into the walls as we passed a convent. I wasn't sure how much of this came from books loaned to me by members of my new congregation and how much was a reaction to my strained and now failed relationship with Sian. In keeping with her gentle manner, she didn't confront me directly but expressed her dismay as she perceived that my faith was less personal, more institutional than she had thought. To use psychological jargon, I was not the self-directed person she thought me to be but was even more other-directed than the most conventional Main Street pew-sitter. To her, Worldwide was just another organization of men, a collection of individuals, most of whom, she assured me, would let me down. I saw it differently. To me, I had transitioned from faith in man to a complete surrender to God and his order. "I had finally found the way to live, in the presence of the Lord," as Blind Faith put it in a song released that summer. It's a common saying that love is blind, but so is conversion. Many years later, when I finally read Thomas Merton's *Seven-Storey Mountain*, a book Sian had urged on me in our time together in the hope it would lead me to become Catholic, I saw the same naive certainty I had in the summer of 1969, and well-understood when Merton said in later years "that was somebody else."

I wrestled with the question of how this new life, centered on submission to the will of God, corresponded to my artistic strivings, which seemed the expression of ego. I had heard in my art history course when analyzing a work of art, that questions of who made it and when were less important than analysis of how it was produced. This corresponded to the reigning theory in literary criticism, the so-called "new criticism," in the English courses I took, which sought to exclude biographical elements from its readings. Now, in the 1960s, there was even an anti-author movement, aleatory art. Writers, musicians, visual artists had long sought to by-pass the stifling effect of rational thought on their work, hoping that instinct or inspiration would deliver. Now writers took scissors to their manuscripts, taping them back together in random order. Composers left room in their works for performers to make choices, sometimes these choices depended on chance, randomly dictated. This was alien to me. To be created, I felt, a work must have a creator, one who disciplines himself and gives the work a degree of form. Studying quantum mechanics had shown me that the cause-effect relationships we depend on in the physical world were underlain by nothing more than probabilities. Perhaps there was a correspondence in art.

When I put effort into something, and it turned out well, I felt the joy of creation. The thirst for recognition was another matter. I tried to imagine a way to separate the joy and pride that come from writing a good poem from the reputation of being called, or thinking of oneself, a good poet or songwriter. Was Dylan's retreat from public view after his motorcycle accident, and the diffident release of *John Wesley Harding* his reaction to similar questions, looming larger in his case because of the pressure to be the spokesman for an entire generation?

George Steiner wrote in a book I read at the time, *Tolstoy or Dostoevski*, "no man is more wholly wrought in God's image or more inevitably his challenger than the poet." To the extent that this might be true, it seemed an invitation to the hubris of Lucifer or Faust. Could this be avoided by excluding biography from art? If it would be possible, would it be desirable? Some writers meant more to me than others, not because their work was better, but because I felt a closeness to them. Their works seemed a prismal mirror in which I could see my face and feelings reflected. Their work was good enough to stand on its own, yet seemed at the same time to construct allegories for my unique experience of the world and my struggles for peace of mind.

With this ambivalence plaguing me, it's no surprise that I undertook no follow-up to the opportunity that had seemed to open to us in New York. Andy and I regretted that our songs never received the arrangements we heard in our minds, but I saw enough of the music business from the sidelines in subsequent years to have no feeling that I somehow missed out.

For the summer I took a job at a bookstore Sheldon Cohen opened on Brattle Street in Cambridge, Reading International. Cohen owned the newsstand on the island in the middle of Harvard Square, next to the stairs leading down to the M.T.A. and was popularly known as the mayor of Harvard Square. His new store boasted a prime location, but also sought to set itself apart from the many bookstores in Cambridge by supplementing a well-selected stock of books with a wall of magazines in many languages. With my knowledge of German and French, my special task was to look after these, in addition to general work. The store also offered photocopying. In those days, not every office had a Xerox machine, and our store had a large one with new features such as collating. In addition to languages, my other special gift was understanding this machine, and getting it running when it was temperamental, saving many service calls.

The location gave my co-workers and me the thrill of spotting celebrities. John Updike strolled in one day, for instance, and went straight to where the "U" novels would be stocked. And I sold George Wald a copy of *The New York Times* with the news article announcing his Nobel prize for biology. One afternoon Julia Child came in with a big copying project, and I chatted with her while I did it, impressed with her non-pretentious enthusiasm for life.

A perk of working there was the chance it afforded to browse through any interesting looking book on my coffee break. I found a quiet corner in the basement for this, nestled among book boxes. Once I got up carelessly and spilled my coffee on the open book I was reading, Jack Newfield's memoir of Bobby Kennedy, which sold well at the time. I put the soiled copy at the bottom of a stack of them with the intention of buying it when payday came around. When I looked for it though, I couldn't find it. I hope that whoever purchased it was able to get a refund (if he or she ever read it).

Another benefit of working there was the partial cure it worked for a lifelong affliction. Growing up surrounded by books created a love of them in me, but also a sense of oppression that there was so much to read. A summer of unloading dozens of boxes at a time from delivery trucks, unpacking them, stacking shelves, and browsing rewarded me with two insights. One was that there were so many books that a lifetime of furious reading wouldn't do more than dent the stack. The second was even more comforting: most weren't worth reading anyway.

The routine of reading, writing, work and Sabbath services was interrupted in the middle of August. Charley had moved out of the apartment; to replace him, Andy and I took in Ron, a classmate who, like Charley, worked at the college radio station. One day he came home with a press pass for a music festival to be held near Woodstock. Everyone at the station had already made summer plans—would I be interested in going?

When the time came, I left work a little early on Friday afternoon and drove to my parents' home in New Jersey. The next day I attended services in the nearby Worldwide congregation for the first time but didn't tell anyone at services where I would be going the next day.

My parents knew, and the first news coverage of the festival made them apprehensive, but they couldn't talk me out of going. The next morning I made some sandwiches with cold steak from the night before, took some apples and a bottle of water, and drove north. Traffic moved smoothly as the Garden State Parkway led to the New York State Thruway. Soon after exiting to Route 17, though, it grew heavier, then bogged down as I approached Bethel, where the festival had been moved at the last minute when Woodstock rescinded its permit. I was still a few miles from the site when I abandoned my car on the side of the road and walked the rest of the way.

It was no problem finding my destination as I set out; I only needed to follow the sound from the large loudspeakers on high scaffolding that flanked the stage. Joe Cocker had begun his set as I made my way through the crowd with my press pass, provisions, and camera stowed in my backpack. I arrived at the side of the stage, was admitted inside the chain link fence that defined where backstage started, and waited my turn to get some stage photos. Toward the end of Cocker's set, I was let onto the photographer's ledge on the wooden stockade fence in front of the stage. In one edit of the Woodstock film, I later caught a brief glimpse of myself there in my blue chambray shirt.

The climax of Cocker's set was his rendition of Lennon and McCartney's "With a Little Help from My Friends." As the Grease Band went into their extended rave-up finish, I cast a side glance at a thundercloud rapidly approaching from the west. It seemed to make a direct line for the stage, then stop. No sooner had Cocker and his band finished than a violent downpour began. I felt as if it were a divine comment on the Dionysian celebration below; perhaps the explanation was simpler, and the electromagnetic charge from the high speaker towers attracted it.

From where I stood, it was easy to take shelter under the stage. I ended up in the middle of goats brought by members of a commune. Although little water came through the plywood sheeting of the stage above, the ground below soon became a sea of mud, since the stage was built at the bottom of a sloping hill. I was at the end of a roll of film and fumbled taking it out of my camera, losing it in the mud. I dug it out, but the film was ruined.

After the rain had stopped, the music resumed, with Country Joe and the Fish taking the stage, and me back on the photographers' ledge. By this time my turn was up, but before leaving the ledge, I turned my camera to photograph the crowd. My best photo from that weekend was of fans in front of the stage, rather than performers on it. Down from the ledge, I wandered through the crowded backstage area filled with faces known or half-familiar in the gathering twilight. Sly Stone called me over to help push a car stuck in the mud, after which I looked for a place to sit down to eat and found one on the steps of a trailer with Joan Baez and Stephen Stills. I offered to share my sandwiches. Baez, six-months pregnant, turned up her nose, but Stills gratefully accepted and enjoyed his portion (Charlie grilled a good steak). I was thrilled at mingling with stars, but they deflected; the real story, I was repeatedly told, was out in front of the stage. Hundreds of thousands had shared an improvised weekend together, overwhelming the systems designed to care for a crowd one-tenth the size and not quite ready because of the last-minute change in the site. The atmosphere had overwhelmingly been that advertised on the posters in advance: three days of peace, love, and music.

By this time, Ten Years After had taken the stage, but I only passively took in the music. My mind was overloaded. My struggles with taming the hubris involved in creativity churned with my awe of these musicians. While they wanted to be admired and respected for what they were, human beings who had worked hard at their craft, they didn't want to be worshiped. As I walked away from the light of the performer's compound to let my impressions sink in, five men came to the crest of a low hill I was walking toward. It was the Band, whom I had seen four years earlier backing Dylan, dressed and ready to go on stage, now looking very much like the photo on the inside of the LP they put out the next winter. I just took it in. Five men who were very skilled at what they did, on their way to work.

Ten Years After finished their set; there was a lull before the next group came on stage. Their last song had been "Going Home," and it was time for me to do that. I had promised to be back in time for work Monday morning, it was now nearly 10 p.m., and I still had to walk an hour to get back to my car, then make the four-hour drive. I retraced my steps from nine hours earlier; the last sounds I heard from the giant speakers behind me were those of the Band, playing the opening chords of "Chest Fever."

I found my car in the dark, maneuvered it out of its place and turned it around. Sometime after getting back on the Thruway the exhaustion hit, and I pulled into a rest stop for a nap; I was sleeping deeply when a nightstick tapping on the window woke me, and a state trooper told me to move on.

The sun had risen as I approached Boston; I went to my apartment, took a quick shower, and headed across the river, only a little late for work, but my co-workers were surprised to see me at all after what they had heard on the news. From their reaction and queries, it seemed as if I had not simply returned from a music festival but a mythical kingdom; had re-ascended from the depths of the earth.

What treasure had I discovered? I enjoyed the attention but was at a loss to know what it meant, other than that my quest was far from over. A child of God, walking along the road.

Henry Sturcke, born in New Jersey, studied photojournalism at Boston University and theology at Ambassador College, Pasadena. After stints as a correspondent in Brussels and Washington, he was ordained as a minister of the Worldwide Church of God, a strict fundamentalist sect living in expectation of the imminent end of the world. He served congregations in Canada, the U. S., Germany, and Switzerland before resigning and earning a Th. D. at the University of Zürich, after which he entered the ministry of the Reformed Church in Switzerland.

You can follow Henry on Facebook and Goodreads.

Henry Sturcke is also the author of *Encountering the Rest of God: How Jesus Came to Personify the Sabbath*, Theologischer Verlag Zürich, 2005. ISBN 978-3290173517

"An excellent piece of scholarship, written in an eminently clear and readable style. It offers a fresh and nuanced perspective on the early development of Christian worship" (Karina Martin Hogan, Fordham University, *Catholic Biblical Quarterly* 68, 2006).

"Recommended to all interested in early Christian worship and history" (Boris Repschinski, Leopold Franzens Universität, Innsbruck, *Review of Biblical Literature*, July 2006).

"An invaluable addition to the library of anyone seeking an authoritative, comprehensive treatment of the scriptural issues surrounding the marginalization of Christian Sabbath observance" (Gavin Rumney, www.otagosh.nz).